AN IN-DEPTH STUDY OF

# FOLLOW
# ME

THE GOSPEL OF
## MATTHEW

E L I Z A B E T H   B A G W E L L   F I C K E N

MW00804600

Follow Me © Copyright 2011, 2016 by Elizabeth Bagwell Ficken
Printed in the United States of America
First Printing, 2011
W & E Publishing, Cary, NC

Scripture quotations identified as NKJV are from the Holy Bible,
*New King James Version*, copyright © 1979, 1980, 1982, Thomas Nelson, Inc.
Publishers. Used by permission. All rights reserved.

Scripture quotations identified NASB are from the
*New American Standard Bible* © The Lockman Foundation, 1960, 1962, 1963,
1968, 1971, 1972, 1973, 1975, 1977. Used by permission.

Scripture quotations identified NIV are from the *New International Version*,
copyright © 1973, 1978, 1984 by International Bible Society.

Scripture quotations identified NLT are from the Holy Bible,
*New Living Translation*, copyright © 1996. Used by permission of
Tyndale House Publishers, Inc., Wheaton, Illinois 60189. All rights reserved.

"Do you know Jesus?" Gospel presentation from Sonlife Classic.
Copyright © 2009 Used by permission.

Cover: Michal Rudolph

*Special thanks to my kindergarten teacher, whose presentation of the
gospel prompted me to ask Jesus to be my Savior. I don't know her name
but I look forward to a very special reunion with her in Heaven one day.*

*Many thanks to Linda Walters for proofreading with excellence.*

*Unending thanks to Jesus Christ who died in my place, forgave my sins,
gave me life through His Holy Spirit so that I could follow Him.*

*Then Jesus said to His disciples, "If anyone desires to come after Me,
let him deny himself, and take up his cross, and follow Me."* **Matthew 16:24**

ISBN-10: 0-9905933-4-7
ISBN-13: 978-0-9905933-4-8

# TABLE OF CONTENTS

# INTRODUCTION

*Dear Friend,*

*How well do you know Jesus? How much time have you spent getting to know Him? Have you immersed yourself in the accounts of His life and His teachings? I heard a seminary professor say that the life of Christ is one of the most neglected subjects of the church. That doesn't make much sense does it?*

*I didn't realize how lacking I was in my own pursuit of knowing Jesus until I began studying the book of Matthew. I realized that I had never studied it or the other gospels before. I've read them many, many times. I've seen the Jesus movie. I've sung the songs about His life and I've even participated in my youth choir's version of the musical Godspell. My pastor preached for at least a year or two straight out of the book of John — verse by verse. But I had never slowed down on my own and actually studied the Scriptures recording the words and works of my Lord Jesus Christ.*

*So I can't say to you that I wrote this study on the book of Matthew because I knew it so well or because it was my favorite gospel. But one day sometime in 2005, the Lord led me to realize that I was supposed to write a study on Matthew. I've got "my list" of books of the Bible on which I would like to write studies. Matthew wasn't on my list. (Every time I think I'm picking a book of the Bible about which to write a study, God points me in another direction!)*

*But I couldn't be happier about God's plan! Four years after becoming aware of God's plan regarding a study on Matthew, I actually began the process. It was extremely challenging, overwhelming, and humbling to realize that I would be handling the sermons of Jesus. Yet it has been an incredible blessing to become intimately acquainted with everything that He said and did with His disciples and everyone He encountered.*

*I am so excited to share a journey with you through the life and teachings of Jesus Christ as presented by Matthew. We're going straight to the source to learn what it really means to be a citizen of the kingdom of heaven. Real discipleship — real Christianity — is explained by and expected from Jesus.*

*What would Jesus do? We love to ask that question; but unless we spend a lot of time with Jesus, we just won't know. So please come with me and let's spend time with Him together. He wants us to follow Him.*

# DO YOU KNOW JESUS?

This is the most important question in this study. Please notice that I didn't ask you if you know about Jesus. But do you know Him, personally?

**The Bible teaches that God loves you.**
"For God so loved the world . . . that He gave His one and only son that whoever believes in Him will not perish, but have eternal life." John 3:16 ESV

**And it teaches that God wants you to know Him personally.**
"Now this is eternal life, that men may know Him, the only true God, and Jesus Christ whom He has sent." John 17:3 ESV

**But . . . people are separated from God by their sin.**
"Your sinful acts have alienated you from your God" Isaiah 59:2 NET

**Sin causes us to miss the very best for our life.**
"Jesus said, 'I came that you might have life and have it to the full." John 10:10 NIV

**Sin causes us to face death and judgment.**
"The wages of sin is death." Romans 3:32 NAS
"Those who do not know God . . . will pay the penalty of eternal destruction away from the presence of the Lord." 2 Thessalonians 1:8-9 NAS

**But there is a solution! Jesus Christ died and conquered death for you! We deserve death and judgment, but Jesus took upon Himself the punishment for our sins, so that we could have a personal relationship with God.**
"For there is only one God and one Mediator who can reconcile God and humanity-- the man Christ Jesus. He gave his life to purchase freedom for everyone." 1 Timothy 2:5-6 NLT

**It's not enough just to know this. Each of us by faith must receive Jesus Christ if we want to know God personally.**
"To all who have received Him—those who believe in His name—He has given the right to become God's children." John 1:12 NET "For it is by grace you have been saved, through faith— and this not from yourselves, it is the gift of God." Ephesians 2:8 NIV

**The ABC's of faith involve:**
Acknowledging your need—admitting you have sinned and desiring to turn from sin. (1 John 1:8-9)
Believing Jesus Christ died in your place and rose again to be your Savior—providing forgiveness for your sins. (1 Corinthians 15:3-4:17)
Choosing to invite Christ to direct your life. (Romans 10:9)

**Your desire to have a personal relationship with God can be expressed through a simple prayer like this:** "Dear Lord, I want to know You personally. Thank you for sending Jesus who died in my place and rose again to be my Savior. Please forgive my sins. I am willing, with your help, to turn from my sins. Come into my life and lead me. Amen."

*For illustrations and more information, go to KnowHimPersonally.com*

# HELPFUL HINTS

**If you are new to in-depth Bible study.** You will need a Bible. Please feel free to use the version of your choice. There are many translations. If you are using a Catholic Bible or a Jewish Old Testament it will be helpful for you to also use a modern version of the Bible which includes the Old and New Testament.

I recommend the following versions which are available for free at online Bible study websites, in smartphone and tablet apps (see recommendations on the next page), or for purchase in Christian bookstores. They are usually referred to by the letters in parentheses.

New King James Version (NKJV)  New American Standard Version (NASB)
New International Version (NIV)  Holman Christian Standard Bible (HCSB)
English Standard Version (ESV)

This study was written using multiple translations. I have found that I can gain understanding of the meaning of verses by reading other versions of the same passage. Two other popular Bibles are *The Message* and the New Living Translation (NLT); these are both wonderful versions for comparative reading, but are not as appropriate for in-depth study.

**Planning time for your lesson.** Set aside a specific amount of time to work on the lesson. One lesson may take 30-40 minutes depending on your familiarity with the Scriptures. You may want to do the lessons in shorter increments of time, depending on your schedule and personal preferences. I find that I absorb, retain, and apply the message of the Scriptures better when I am not rushed.

**Please begin your study time with prayer.** Ask the Holy Spirit to give you understanding of God's Word, as it is promised that He will do according to 1 Corinthians 2:12-13: "Now we have received, not the spirit of the world, but the Spirit who is from God, that we might know the things freely given to us by God, which things we also speak, not in words taught by human wisdom, but in those taught by the Spirit, combining spiritual thoughts with spiritual words." I have given you a reminder at the beginning of each lesson.

**Observation, interpretation, and application.** The Scripture readings, activities, cross-references and word definitions are all placed in the order which is most appropriate to your study. It is best to follow this order if you can, rather than skipping steps or setting steps aside to be completed at a different time. The order follows the inductive study process: observation (what the Scripture says), interpretation (what the author intended, what the Scripture means) and application (what difference the Scripture makes in your life). You will be doing the research, cross-referencing and summarization of the truths of each passage. When you finish a study of a passage, you will have gleaned more understanding on your own than you will find in some commentaries!

**Looking up Greek word definitions.** One of the activities included to help you understand the correct interpretation of the scripture is discovering and considering the definition of a word in its original language. Please make sure that you look up the definition of the word in its original language, not the definition of the English word. You will be given a prompt like this:

**Faith: Strong's #4102**
**Greek word:**
**Greek definition:**

There are several ways you can look up the words given.

- You can google the Strong's reference number (Strong's 4102) and your web browser will give you links to the definition.
- You can go to an online Bible study website (recommendations below) and use their free reference materials. Look for "study" tabs, "lexicons" (this is what Hebrew and Greek word dictionaries are called), "concordances" and "original language" tools. There are search boxes where you can type in the Strong's reference number. Use G before the number for Greek words (G4102).

  **studylight.org     blueletterbible.com     searchgodsword.org**

  Suggested resources, described on page 178, are also available at these websites if you want to do more research on your own.
- You can download free Bible study apps for your smartphone and/or tablet. I use **MySword** which allows me to go to a passage and click on the Strong's reference number next to the word. Try a few different ones and see what you like best.
- You may have some great resources on your own bookshelves! Enjoy using books like: *Strong's Exhaustive Concordance* and *The Complete Word Study Dictionary* by Spiros Zhodiates.

If you have trouble, it would be better to skip the exercise rather than filling in the English definition.

**It's about your head and your heart.** My hope is that you will read portions of Scripture and gain understanding of what is being communicated through them so that you can consider how to apply the truth of God's Word to your life. I have tried to make the study "user-friendly" and I promise that I don't ask trick questions. I do want to make you think hard sometimes though! I hope you won't get overwhelmed. Do what you can, a little bit at a time. The reward of knowing our holy God through His recorded word far outweighs the time and effort of study.

**Prayer requests and praises.** You will find pages at the end of this workbook which provide prompts from Scriptures for your prayers as well as a place for you to write out a personal prayer request . If you are studying with a group, it would be helpful to reflect on your personal prayer request before sharing it with the group. Keep your requests brief and personal. This page is also a place to record the prayer requests of others.

# MY BIBLE STORY

*I love my Bible! But I have about 10 of them on my bookshelf, so which one do I love and use to read and study? I'd like to answer that question with my Bible story.*

*The earliest Bible that I remember reading was a children's New Testament Living Bible. It was a birthday present from a friend when I was eight years old! I tried to read the book of Revelation, but didn't get very far. The next special Bible that I received was a black (faux) leather King James Version with Susan Elizabeth Bagwell engraved in gold letters on the front. This was from my parents, and it was my church Bible. I don't remember reading it at all, but I must have taken it to Sunday School with me because I found a Psalm 23 bookmark in it. That was to become the first well-known Scripture to me.*

*When I was fourteen I began using a paperback Bible which my father felt was an excellent translation. The New English Bible is not very well known, but it was the Bible that helped me begin to know God's Word. My Sunday school teacher actually made us read and study Ephesians so I began taking this Bible to church. I also underlined verses and took it with me to Bible studies in high school.*

*My first Bible with cross-references and helpful notes was the Ryrie Study Bible in the King James Version. A friend took me to the Baptist Bookstore, and I experienced picking out a Bible for myself. It was bound in dark blue leather and Elizabeth Bagwell was engraved in silver lettering. I bought it after high school graduation and used it for my quiet times and Bible study and sermon notes for about 10 years—through college and early marriage and the births of my children! It was falling apart and the bookbinder recommended a durable covering: blue canvas. I call it my blue jean Bible now!*

*Then I became aware of the New King James Version and decided it would be nice to leave behind the Thee's and Thou's of the Old King James . . . so I bought The Woman's Study Bible NJKV. It was refreshing to read God's truths in a new translation in a Bible that had clean pages where I could make new notes. Familiar verses were lovely and overlooked verses began to stand out as they had not done before. The changing of Bible translations became a new adventure for me.*

*I own and have read through the Bible in the NIV, NLT, NET, NAS, NKJ, ESV, and I'm currently reading through the HCSB. It is important to me to have a Bible with helpful study notes: historical and cultural information; word study definitions; maps; and appropriate cross-references. The layout of the Scriptures on the pages is important too! It just has to feel right! I have used the Archeological Study Bible and the Life Application Bible, but have enjoyed the Nelson Study Bible and the Holman Christian Standard Study Bible more.*

*Jesus loves me this I know, for my Bible tells me so! I love God's Word and I love my Bible—whichever one I may be reading at any given time.*

# UNIT ONE  MATTHEW 1:1 — 5:1

LESSON 1  JESUS' GENEALOGY

LESSON 2  JESUS' BIRTH

LESSON 3  JESUS' BAPTISM

LESSON 4  JESUS VERSUS SATAN

LESSON 5  JESUS' MESSAGE

LESSON 6  JESUS' SERMON ON THE MOUNTAIN

# JESUS' GENEALOGY

"The Gospel According to Matthew" has been called by many Bible scholars the most important single document of the Christian faith. Historians tell us that this book was the most widely read, and the most quoted, in the early church.[1]

*That surprises and fascinates me! What about you? There are many other books in the Bible that I would have expected to be more important to our Christian faith. Through our study of Matthew, we will come to understand its crucial contribution to understanding who Jesus Christ is. Matthew's purpose for writing his book will become crystal clear. And while we are learning incredible theological truths, we will also become intimately acquainted with Jesus as we look at His life on earth, His power, His authority, His miracles, and above all - His teaching. The book of Matthew contains more of Jesus' sermons and teachings than the other three gospels, with His words making up about 60 percent of the book.*

*Our study will be an exciting and challenging adventure as we follow the steps of Jesus through the land of Israel. We will roam the desert wilderness, climb mountains, cross the Sea of Galilee, and visit the Temple in Jerusalem. We will also meet people from all walks of life and watch their response to Jesus. Men, women, children, rich, poor, sick, demon-possessed, fishermen and Pharisees, the elite and the under-class. They either love Him or hate Him, but they can't ignore Him!*

*I'm eager to begin our study, but I can't begin without turning to our Father in Heaven and asking Him to teach me through His Holy Spirit. Each day, I will prompt you to bow before Him as well making yourself dependent on the Spirit to give you understanding of the Word of God. Let's do that now.*

Please pray that the Holy Spirit will give you a
desire to know Jesus more intimately.

*We'll begin in the beginning – that's in Genesis! Genesis 5:1 says, "This is the book of the genealogy of Adam." From that verse forward through the end of the Old Testament, the story of the family of Adam is told. Adam had sinned; and the rest of his family, his offspring down through the ages, proved themselves to be sinners as well.*

*The New Testament, however, presents the story of the sinless One who came to save sinners. Matthew 1:1 is very similar to Genesis 5:1. It says, "The book of the genealogy of Jesus Christ, the son of David, the son of Abraham."* [NAS] *This is the most shocking, the most fascinating, and the most informative genealogy in the Bible. We could study each individual that is named, but instead we'll stay focused on the most important person of all time.*

*This list is what Matthew thought should have first priority in his account of the gospel. Our study must give it the attention it deserves! The genealogy of Jesus Christ lays the foundation for the rest of the book of Matthew and for our faith.*

**Please read Matthew 1:1-17.**

List the three statements which specifically describe Jesus.

*You have just recorded the most important truth of all time. Matthew's purpose was to present to his readers the evidence that Jesus is the Christ. The rest of the book does just that. Through His teachings, His miracles, His fulfillment of prophecy, His statements about Himself, and the recognition of His identity through men, women, and children, it is proven without a doubt that Jesus is the Christ.*

Please look up the definition for the following word:
**Christ: Strong's #5547**
**Greek word:**
**Greek definition:**

*This word is the equivalent to the Hebrew word "Messiah" which also means "anointed." Why is this such an important concept? We'll have to look back to the Old Testament to find the answer.*

Who is anointed in the following verses?

**Exodus 30:30**

**2 Samuel 12:7**

What did the Lord promise David according to 2 Samuel 7:11-13?

*Following the reign of King David, the nation of Israel watched with anticipation for the Messiah who would be the king who would rule in righteousness and establish a kingdom safe and secure from their enemies.*

Now look back at the genealogy recorded in Matthew 1:1-17. How often is David's name mentioned? What does this indicate?

Look at the following verses and note who spoke and what they said.

**Matthew 9:27**

**Matthew 12:23**

**Matthew 15:22**

**Matthew 20:30**

**Matthew 21:9, 15**


*Matthew's book has been called "the gospel of the King." Jesus' right to the throne is demonstrated through being a direct descendant of King David. We will soon see that He knew that He was the King and had come to usher in His kingdom.*

*Not only did Matthew give evidence that Jesus was a descendant of David, he also emphasized that Jesus was the Christ.*

Record what is stated in the following verses:

**Matthew 2:4**

**Matthew 11:2**

**Matthew 16:16, 20**

**Matthew 22:42**

**Matthew 23:8, 10**

**Matthew 26:63-64**

**Matthew 27:17, 22**


*You have just seen the basic purpose of the book of Matthew: to explain that Jesus is the anticipated Messiah, the Son of David, the Anointed King, the Christ. But there is more! The book of Matthew records Jesus' teachings on His kingdom which is the kingdom of heaven on earth. And it also shows that the nation of Israel either didn't recognize Jesus as King or rejected Him as such - while Gentiles and even demons responded to His authority.*

*I'd like to mention to you at this point that Matthew did not record a chronological account of Jesus' life. This could "vex and perplex" you, as someone else put it! There is a beautiful harmony to the gospels, but sometimes it seems more like one of the authors struck the wrong note. It will be helpful to realize that Matthew's book is arranged thematically, with five distinct sections framed by Jesus' birth (Matt. 1:1 – 2:23) and death (Matt. 26:2 – 28:20).*

*These five sections contain Jesus' sermons, His instructions, and His teachings. I think it is quite interesting that Matthew arranged his book so that the words of Jesus are presented in five sections, just as the first words of God in the Old Testament are in five sections, the first five books of the Bible. This structure shows that Jesus' words are God's words!*

Look at the following outline of the book of Matthew, and fill in the blanks with the transitional statement where indicated.

**Introduction: Matthew 1:1 – 4:11** – Genealogy, Birth, Baptism, Temptation

**Section 1: Matthew 4:12 – 7:29** – The Sermon on the Mount

Transitional statement: Matthew 7:28: _____

_____

**Section 2: Matthew 8:1 – 11:1** – The Commissioning of the Apostles

Transitional statement: Matthew 11:1 _____

_____

**Section 3: Matthew 11:2 – 13:52** – The Parables of the Kingdom

Transitional statement: Matthew 13:53_____

_____

**Section 4: Matthew 13:53 – 19:1** – The Childlikeness of the Believer

Transitional statement: Matthew 19:1 _____

_____

**Section 5: Matthew 19:2 – 26:1** – The Olivet Discourse: His Second Coming

Transitional statement: Matthew 26:1 _____

_____

**Conclusion: Matthew 26:1 – 28:20** Jesus' Death and Resurrection

Do you see from these verses that Matthew emphasized the teachings of Jesus? How do you feel about embarking on a study of the very words of Jesus the Christ?

> Happy ye, whose eyes and ears, voluntarily and gladly opened, are drinking in the light divine.[2]

You've now had your first look at the book of Matthew. I hope you have been blessed by what you've seen! Please write Matthew 13:16.

*I'd like to encourage you once again to read the genealogy of Jesus the Christ and review your notes.*

What, if anything, did the Lord show you today?

---

Lesson Two: Matthew 1:18-2:23

# JESUS' BIRTH

*I hope your Christmases have been filled with the meaningful tradition of reading the account of Jesus' birth. I am thankful that both my husband and I come from families that honor the Lord and on December 25 emphasize the celebration of His miraculous birth. It has been wonderful to hear our children and nieces and nephews recite portions of the Christmas story.*

*But the account of Jesus' birth is not just for the Christmas season. Such a thing didn't even exist when Matthew recorded this great event. So let's read it today and discover the important details that continue to introduce the person of Jesus — the details that are miraculous, amazing, and life-changing!*

> Please pray that the Holy Spirit will open your eyes to the majesty of the birth of the Christ.

**Please read Matthew 1:18-2:23 in its entirety.**

What stands out to you in a special way as you read this account today?

Please list each way that Jesus is described in these verses.

*In the previous lesson, you looked up the very important title by which Jesus is known, the Christ, and saw that it means: the Anointed One, the Messiah, the long-awaited King. Now let's look at the very significant name that Joseph was commanded to give to Mary's child.*

Please look up the following words:
**Jesus: Strong's #2424**
**Greek word:**
**Greek definition:**

**Hebrew origin of Jesus: Strong's #3091**
**Hebrew word:**
**Hebrew definition:**

*The gospel of salvation through faith in Jesus is already being preached in the account of His birth! Jesus – what a wonderful name.*

Who will be saved from their sin, according to Matthew 1:21?

*It will be made very clear through the whole book of Matthew that Jesus came to His own people and preached His message of salvation to them first. God keeps His promises to His chosen nation of Israel. But it will also be made very clear that the rest of the world can receive salvation as well.*

*While there are many supernatural occurrences in the story of Jesus' birth, there are a few statements recorded to which we must pay close attention.*

**According to Matthew 1:18-25:**
How did Mary become pregnant?

How can we be sure that Joseph was not the biological father?

Why did all this happen, according to Matthew?

*"'Behold, the virgin shall be with child, and bear a Son, and they shall call His name Immanuel,' which is translated 'God with us.'" Matthew quotes Isaiah 7:14 and begins to prove from the Old Testament that Jesus is the Messiah, the King, who is the Son of God. He makes the profound declaration that Jesus, who is a human being, is also God Himself in the flesh. This was a critical concept that was extremely controversial during Jesus' life and is just as controversial today.*

Do you believe that Jesus was fully man and fully God?

Do you know anyone who does not believe this?

Why is it so important to understand that Jesus was fully God and fully man?

*Wow! Will we ever really be able to grasp this incredible truth? The fact that Jesus was fully man and fully God astounds me. I believe it though, and my life today and my life for eternity depend on this truth.*

> "The eternal Son of the eternal God had existed as One with the Father from all eternity. The One who by His power had created the universe would come in human flesh through Mary's womb. Jesus Christ, the eternal One, reached out through His birth and took to Himself a true and complete humanity. He united true humanity and true deity in one person forever. Such was the revelation given to Joseph."[3]

Hebrews 2:14-18 explains this concept and the impact that it has on our lives. What do you learn from verses 17 and 18?

*It's only the second lesson in our study of the life of Christ, and we are contemplating an extremely deep concept! I'm moved to worship the newborn King just as the wise men were.*

Please read through Matthew 1:18-2:23 again.

*The Messiah, the Savior, the King of the Jews, the Son of God was born. Joseph accepted it. Herod hated it. The wise men believed it.*

What is your reaction?

Matthew emphasizes four fulfillments of prophecy in his narrative of Jesus' birth. Please summarize the prophecies in the following verses:

**Matthew 2:5-6** (fulfilled Micah 5:2)

**Matthew 2:15** (fulfilled Hosea 11:1)

**Matthew 2:17-18** (fulfilled Jeremiah 31:15)

**Matthew 2:23** (summary of Old Testament teachings that the Messiah would be despised and rejected, i.e. Psalm 22, Isaiah 53:3; Nazareth was a place held in contempt)

> "Matthew was noting that every incident that took place in the life of Christ was in keeping with the Old Testament prophetic Scriptures. This was true whether the incident fulfilled a direct prophecy, such as concerning the place of His birth [Matt. 2:6], whether it fulfilled a prophetic type [Matt. 2:15], or whether it fulfilled a prophecy according to the principle of double reference [Matt. 2:17 – 18]. All took place in accordance with the revealed program of God." [4]

What impact does it have on you to see that specific prophecies were fulfilled in Jesus' life? Do you expect to see Scriptures fulfilled in your own life?

*Chapters One and Two of Matthew have introduced Jesus to us as the rightful heir to the throne of David, as the long-awaited Messiah, as the Son of God conceived by the Holy Spirit, and as our King and Savior. The events surrounding Jesus' birth show us that God is in control, carrying out His eternal plan, and revealing His will to His servants.*

*Let us join the heavenly host with their praises to God! "Glory to God in the highest, and on earth peace among men with whom He is pleased!" Luke 2:14 [NAS]*

Lesson Three: Matthew 3:1-17

## JESUS' BAPTISM

*"Many years later, after Jesus reached adulthood, he went out to see his cousin John who was in the desert baptizing those who were repenting of their sins." That would have been a nice transition for Matthew to give us between Chapters 2 and 3! But he didn't. At the beginning of Chapter 3, we have an abrupt shift from the description of Jesus' birth to a description of John the Baptist.*

*Isn't Matthew's focus on Jesus the Messiah? Oh yes it is, and that is exactly why he includes the person and perspective of John. John makes sure that we concern ourselves with who the Messiah is and what He does. And then Matthew concludes his account with a shocking, dramatic event full of supernatural special effects.*

*Let's see what we are to learn from Matthew 3.*

Pray that you will understand the importance
of the following events.

**Please read Matthew 3:1-12.**

Just who is John the Baptist and what is he all about? Describe him and his mission based on the passage you just read.

*The three other gospels also present John the Baptist as the important forerunner to Jesus. His birth is described in Luke 1. Mark 1:3-8 and Luke 3:2-17 summarize his ministry in the wilderness just as Matthew does, almost word for word. He had the same lifestyle and radical message as that of an Old Testament prophet. Elijah was his role model in many ways, including the way he dressed (2 Kings 1:8)! The gospel of John condenses his role into three short verses.*

How does John 1:6-8 describe John the Baptist?

*As John bore witness that the Messiah was coming, he urged the people to prepare for Him by repenting of their sins. Repent and be baptized – for the kingdom of heaven is at hand. This was his message.*

> The Greek word *baptize* comes from the root *bapto,* which literally means to dip or to dye. It was a common word among those in the fuller's trade. Undressed cloth was prepared for use by first dipping it into bleach and then into dye. The emphasis...in the word is not on the procedure of dipping but rather on the result of the procedure. The cloth woven of unprocessed sheep's wool was dull and it needed to be cleansed. The appearance of the cloth was changed by putting the cloth into the bleach and then into dye. When it emerged from the bleach, it was clean and white; and when it emerged from the dye, its appearance was further altered....The word metaphorically means to change identity, to change appearance, or even to change relationships.[5]

*Repent and be baptized. It's the very message that Jesus Himself preached. "From that time Jesus began to preach and say, 'Repent, for the kingdom of heaven is at hand.'" Matthew 4:17.* [NAS] *The kingdom of heaven is a very important concept in the book of Matthew. We'll consider it more closely in another lesson.*

**Please read Matthew 3:7-10 and answer the following questions:**

Who is being addressed in this passage?

How are they described?

*The Pharisees and Sadducees were the religious leaders of the times. These two distinct groups made up the council known as the Sanhedrin. The Pharisees were connected with local synagogues; they studied the Law of the Old Testament and adhered strictly to the oral interpretations of the Law and to their ancestral traditions. The Pharisees represented the broad masses of the Jewish people. The Sadducees, on the other hand, were a small aristocratic group from which came the powerful High Priest. They did not believe in life after death or the resurrection of the body, or in future punishment as part of judgment.*

In the passage you just read, how does John rebuke these two groups?

*The ax is lying at the root of the trees. The time will come when the Judge will pick up the ax and chop down each tree that does not bear good fruit. The rest of John's message tells of the hope of those who repent and the horror of those who don't.*

What is the hope and the promise for those who repent, according to Matthew 3:11-12?

What is the horror to come for those who do not repent, according to Matthew 3:11-12?

*Which would you choose? I hope you have already made your choice and that you are ready for the arrival of the King.*

If you have repented of your sins and trusted in Jesus as the One who forgives your sins, what is the truth declared in Ephesians 1:13-14?

*Obeying the word of God by the power of the Holy Spirit — that's how we are to live our lives. It was first modeled to us by Jesus Himself, as we will see in the next passage.*

*I'd like to show you the impact that the nuances of the Greek language make on a few sentences. I hope it will help you see what was out of the ordinary in this event. The italicized phrases are literal Greek translations, and the bold font expresses an imperative command.*

**Please read Matthew 3:13-17 quoted below.**

"Then Jesus *Himself* came…and John tried to prevent Him saying, '*I have a need* to be baptized by You'…but Jesus said, '**Permit it now**….' After Jesus had been baptized… *behold!*… the heavens were opened and he saw the Spirit of God descending like a dove and alighting on Him. And *behold!* a voice came from heaven, saying, 'This is My beloved Son, in whom I am well pleased.'"

Looking at your Bible and the translation above, describe the surprising aspects of this event:
Verses 13-14

Verse 15

Verse 16

Verse 17

*Do these things surprise you? That Jesus came to be baptized? That the Holy Spirit came upon Him? That God spoke? These are the very things that Matthew emphasized in this account. Why did Jesus need to be baptized? Did He receive the Holy Spirit at this time? Had Jesus done something to make His heavenly Father pleased with Him? Let's consider these questions.*

Why did Jesus say He was to be baptized? (You don't have to explain it, just record what He said.)

*I think this is hard to understand! The key is understanding how Matthew used the word righteousness. We need to remember throughout our study of his book that he was a Jew, writing for a Jewish audience. Some even say that this gospel was first written in Hebrew then translated into Greek. Matthew would have understood the Hebrew concepts of the words he used.*

*In the Old Testament, the word for righteousness is "tsedeqah" and it comes from the root word which basically means to conform to an ethical or moral standard.*[6] *The Greek word "diakesoune" then, in Matthew's context means: what God requires; what is right; religious duties or acts of charity.*[7] *So Jesus was telling John, "You must baptize me because it is the right thing to do. It is what God wants."*

How do you respond when you are given instructions that you don't quite understand? Do you submit to the ways of the Lord even when they don't make sense to you?

*Commentators say that Jesus' baptism gave approval to John's ministry and linked the two ministries together, providing the transition from the one to the other. It was time for Jesus to be in the spotlight. It was time for a supernatural revelation of who He was.*

What does Isaiah 11:1-2 tell you about the Holy Spirit?

What does John 1:32-34 tell you about the Holy Spirit coming upon Jesus?

*Jesus had been conceived by the Holy Spirit and therefore had been filled with the Spirit from the womb but His baptism was a special ceremony. The conclusion to this spectacular event is an announcement from heaven. It reflects two messianic passages from the Old Testament.*

How does Matthew 3:17 relate to Psalm 2:7 and Isaiah 42:1?

*Behold! The voice of the Lord! Jesus had not even begun His ministry, but God the Father was pleased with Him and declared His love for Him. Jesus was the Son, the Servant, and the Beloved. He had already demonstrated obedience in fulfilling all righteousness. He was anointed with the Spirit and empowered to begin His mission. The first three chapters of Matthew make it clear that Jesus was no ordinary man.*

Lesson Four: Matthew 4:1-11

## JESUS VERSUS SATAN

*Today we will look at the first recorded challenge to Jesus' mission on earth. The enemy of God is always out to wreak havoc in the lives of God's children, and he made no exception for Jesus. The Son of God was the ultimate target. If Satan could make Jesus disobey His Father, he would win the eternal victory. But Matthew doesn't even give us a hint of anxiety regarding this event. With a very matter of fact account of the temptation of Jesus, he shows us that the enemy of God is no match for the Son of God.*

Please pray to know and live by the word of God.

**Please read Matthew 4:1-11.** What's the first word of the passage? (I've checked all the translations and they are the same… even in the Greek!) First word: _____

That word makes this passage connected to what previous event? And what was the crucial revelation given at that event?

Now we are ready to continue…please fill in the following blanks as we notice a few key points in verse 1.

Jesus was led by the _____.

Jesus was led into the _____.

Jesus was led there to be _____ by the _____.

It's easy to fill in those blanks, but let's consider the impact of those statements. What conclusion can you make regarding the role of the Lord and the role of Satan when it comes to temptation?

*Because Jesus endured temptation and escaped from it, His example shows us how to do the same. Let's see what the temptations were and how He handled them.*

Please fill in the columns below based on Matthew 4.

|  | **First attempt** <br> **Matthew 4:2-4** | **Second attempt** <br> **Matthew 4:5-7** | **Third attempt** <br> **Matthew 4:8-10** |
|---|---|---|---|
| **Circumstance** |  |  |  |
| **Temptation** |  |  |  |
| **Response** |  |  |  |

*Was the third time a charm for Satan? No! Jesus did not succumb to his repeated attempts to destroy Him. It was more like – three strikes and you're out!*

*Satan began his temptations with the words, "If you are the Son of God..." (It's implied in the third temptation.) This is critically important and shows the connection to the declaration made at Jesus' baptism. The construction of this sentence in the Greek causes the "if" to mean "since" or "because." Therefore, we should understand that Satan was saying, "Since you are the Son of God..."*

*Satan did not doubt that Jesus was the Son of God. He knew that He was. And he wasn't trying to get Jesus to doubt that He was the Son of God. Satan was trying to get Jesus to take advantage of His own power and to act independently of His Father's will for Him.*

In each circumstance above, who gave a command to Jesus?

And in each circumstance, whose command did Jesus obey?

Whose commands do you listen to in the circumstances of your life?

*It's hard to listen to and obey the commands of the Lord if you don't know them. Jesus demonstrated that knowing the words of the Lord from the Scriptures is the most important aspect of standing firm against temptation.*

What did Jesus declare in each circumstance before stating the command of the Lord?

*The word "written" is in the perfect tense in Matthew 4:4, 7, and 10. My **Basics of Biblical Greek Grammar** book states: "the perfect tense describes an action that was brought to completion and whose effects are felt in the present."* [8]

Summarize what you learn about the Word of God based on these verses and the use of the perfect tense of "written."

*Jesus didn't stand resolutely against the schemes of Satan by His own strength, identity, or authority. He rebuked Satan with the written words of God. How much more so should we rely on the authority of Scripture?*

Time for a pop-quiz! To the best of your ability, write out one verse that you have memorized. You can check your work after you've given it your best effort!

*Words to live by. Words to trust. Words to lead us to worship. We must know the Word of God so that we can follow His commands and none other. This was the way that Jesus became victorious over the enemy and the way that we will as well. Let us learn the truth of the Word of God and apply it appropriately during our times of testing.*

After forty long, hard days and nights, and after three rounds with the tempter, how did Jesus recover?

Now that you've seen the complete plan regarding temptation (Matthew 4:1-11), what will your strategy be before, during, and after times of temptation?

*Jesus' temptation was a testing allowed by the Lord. Jesus was now completely prepared to begin His public ministry. He had obeyed His Father; He had been publicly anointed by the Spirit and announced as the Son of God; and He had withstood the temptations of the enemy. The time had come. The Messiah was about to begin His mission.*

Lesson Five: Matthew 4:12-25

# JESUS' MESSAGE

*The stage is set. The way has been prepared. The introductions have been made. It's time. Jesus the Messiah has a message He will preach and a mission He will carry out. Let's see how He gets started.*

Please prepare for your study today by expressing your dependence on the Spirit to teach you.

**Please read Matthew 4:12-25.**

This passage is full of people and places. List every geographical location that Matthew names and note which region is mentioned the most often.

*Matthew may have been a tax collector, but I think he would have made a good lawyer. He is always proving his case that Jesus is the Messiah with evidence from the Old Testament. He shows once again that Jesus' actions were "that it might be fulfilled which was spoken..."*

How is Galilee described in Matthew 4:15-16?

Please look up the definition of the following word and record what you learn from a Bible dictionary or encyclopedia. (See Suggested Resources, page 240.)

**Gentiles: Strong's #1484**
**Greek word:**
**Greek definition:**

**Bible dictionary notes:**

*Jesus relocated from Judea to the land of the Gentiles and began His ministry there. What a surprise! Do you remember what the angel of the Lord told Joseph? That Jesus will save His people from their sins (Matt. 1:21). His people were Jews, not Gentiles. Oh, but Jesus' sacrifice was big enough for anyone who believes in Him to be saved! Hallelujah!*

What do you learn about salvation for Gentiles from the following verses?

**Isaiah 49:6**

**Luke 2:30-32**

**Ephesians 2:11-13**

What is your response to these truths? What impact do they have on you?

*It is so important for us, here at the beginning of our study of the life of Christ described by Matthew, to understand that Matthew writes to a Jewish audience, proving that Jesus is their Messiah. But he also writes to the Gentile audience, proving that Jesus is their Messiah – their King, their Savior, as well. Jesus' message was not just for one nation under God but for the whole world.*

What was Jesus' message to the whole world, according to Matthew 4:17?


*We've already seen this message preached by John the Baptist. Jesus said the same thing. We will see that throughout His ministry, He will explain the concept of the kingdom of heaven to the people, especially His disciples. This phrase is repeated 32 times in Matthew, with all of chapter 13 explaining the concept through parables.*

We will consider the kingdom of heaven throughout our study of Matthew. For now, what do you learn about it from these verses?

**Matthew 5:3**

**Matthew 5:20**

**Matthew 7:21**

**Matthew 13:11**

**Matthew 13:44**

**Matthew 18:4**

---

We have been introduced to the first important location for Jesus' ministry: "Galilee of the Gentiles" (v.15). We have been introduced to His message: "Repent, for the kingdom of heaven is near" (v.17). Now we are to be introduced to an important part of His methodology: to call disciples he would teach and who would then teach and preach to other people.[9]

---

Summarize the call of the first disciples in Matthew 4:18 – 22 with a headline and a paragraph for a newscast. Be creative! The reporter's questions to be answered are: who, what, when, where, why, and how.


*Are we given any reason for these particular men to be chosen? I don't see any. They are just ordinary men, doing ordinary jobs. But then, Someone extraordinary walked by and gave them an offer they couldn't refuse.*

What was the brief command given by Jesus to the brothers?

*James Montgomery Boice says that these two words teach the following important truths: obedience, repentance, submission, trust, and perseverance.*[10]

Have you heard the call to follow Jesus? Have you responded with your whole being, as the first disciples did? Which, if any, of the important truths above is missing in your following of Jesus today?

*"Follow Me." This command from Jesus is the title of this study and the overall theme of this particular study on Matthew. We are not studying an historical figure or a simple Jew or a royal King just to learn more about someone from the past. My prayer is that our study of the life of Christ and His teachings will help us know Him more personally and truly follow Him as He desires for us to do.*

The disciples weren't the only ones who followed Jesus. Who else followed Jesus and why, according to Matthew 4:23-25?

*This brings us to the end of Matthew's first narrative of Jesus ministry. The crowds have gathered and Jesus is preaching. Soon we will hear what Jesus had to say to them. The kingdom of heaven was at hand, but who could enter in? Jesus explains this to multitudes on the mount. Get ready for a sermon that was shocking!*

Lesson Six: Matthew 5:1-7:29

# JESUS' SERMON ON THE MOUNTAIN

*We are about to study what may be the most important recorded sermon of all time. You can probably recall a few phrases from famous speeches given over the course of history, but no one address has had a greater impact on the world than the Sermon on the Mount. It is about the way we are to live and why we should live that way. Thousands of books and articles and lessons have been taught on these three significant chapters from Matthew.*

*Are you ready to hear Jesus speak? He communicates with wisdom, intensity, truth, and real-life illustrations. This message is personal and passionate. Listen to Him intently as He shares what is of the utmost concern to Him – it's what we need to understand about the kingdom of heaven.*

*I want you to see this message in its entirety. We will spend several lessons studying it in smaller segments, but we must see the whole context to grasp the big picture. You may find yourself so familiar with some of verses that you miss their impact. Try to read with a fresh awareness of what is being said.*

Pray that the Lord will open your eyes to His truths
every time you study His word.

**Please read Matthew 5:1-7:29.** As you read, highlight each occurrence of "the kingdom of heaven," "kingdom," "heaven," "heavenly Father" and "Father in heaven."

**Matthew 5:1 - 7:29:** And seeing the multitudes, He went up on a mountain, and when He was seated His disciples came to Him. [2]Then He opened His mouth and taught them, saying: [3]"Blessed are the poor in spirit, for theirs is the kingdom of heaven. [4]Blessed are those who mourn, for they shall be comforted. [5]Blessed are the meek, for they shall inherit the earth. [6]Blessed are those who hunger and thirst for righteousness, for they shall be filled. [7]Blessed are the merciful, for they shall obtain mercy. [8]Blessed are the pure in heart, for they shall see God. [9]Blessed are the peacemakers, for they shall be called sons of God. [10]Blessed are those who are persecuted for righteousness' sake, for theirs is the kingdom of heaven. [11]Blessed are you when they revile and persecute you, and say all kinds of evil against you falsely for My sake. [12]Rejoice and be exceedingly glad, for great is your reward in heaven, for so they persecuted the prophets who were before you. [13]You are the salt of the earth; but if the salt loses its flavor, how shall it be seasoned? It is then good for nothing but to be thrown out and trampled underfoot by men. [14]You are the light of the world. A city that is set on a hill cannot be hidden. [15]Nor do they light a lamp and put it under a basket, but on a lampstand, and it gives light to all who are in the house. [16]Let your light so shine before men, that they may see your good works and glorify your Father in heaven. [17]Do not think that I came to destroy the Law or the Prophets. I did not come to destroy but to fulfill. [18]For assuredly, I say to you, till heaven and earth pass away, one jot or one tittle will by no means pass from the law till all is fulfilled. [19]Whoever therefore breaks one of the least of these commandments, and teaches men so, shall be called least in the kingdom of heaven; but whoever does and teaches them, he shall be called great in the kingdom of heaven. [20]For I say to you, that unless your righteousness exceeds the righteousness of the scribes and Pharisees, you will by no means enter the kingdom of heaven. [21]You have heard that it was said to those of old, 'You shall not murder, and whoever murders will be in danger of the judgment.' [22]But I say to you that whoever is angry with his brother without a cause shall be in danger of the judgment. And whoever says to his brother, 'Raca!' shall be in danger of the council. But whoever says, 'You fool!' shall be in danger of hell fire. [23]Therefore if you bring your gift to the altar, and there remember that your brother has something against you, [24]leave your gift there before the altar, and go your way. First be reconciled to your brother, and then come and offer your gift. [25]Agree with your adversary quickly, while you are on the way with him, lest your adversary deliver you to the judge, the judge hand you over to the officer, and you be thrown into prison. [26]Assuredly, I say to you, you will by no means get out of there till you have paid the last penny. ²⁷You have heard that it was said to those of old, 'You shall not commit adultery.' ²⁸But I say to you that whoever looks at a woman to lust for her has already committed adultery with her in his heart. ²⁹If your right eye causes you to sin, pluck it out and cast it from you; for it is more profitable for you that one of your members perish, than for your whole body to be cast into hell. ³⁰And if your right hand causes you to sin, cut it off and cast it from you; for it is more profitable for you that one of your members perish, than for your whole body to be cast into hell. ³¹Furthermore it has been said, 'Whoever divorces his wife, let him give her a certificate of divorce.' ³²But I say to you that whoever divorces his wife for any reason except sexual immorality causes her to commit adultery; and whoever marries a woman who is divorced commits adultery. ³³Again you have heard that it was said to those of old, 'You shall not swear falsely, but shall perform your oaths to the Lord.' ³⁴But I say to you, do not swear at all: neither by heaven, for it is God's throne; ³⁵nor by the earth, for it is His footstool; nor by Jerusalem, for it is the city of the great King. ³⁶Nor shall you swear by your head, because you cannot make one hair white or black. ³⁷But let your 'Yes' be 'Yes,' and your 'No,' 'No.' For whatever is more than these is from the evil one. ³⁸You have heard that it was said, 'An eye for an eye and a tooth for a tooth.' ³⁹But I tell you not to resist an evil person. But whoever slaps you on your right cheek, turn the other to him also. ⁴⁰If anyone wants to sue you and take away your tunic, let him have your cloak also. ⁴¹And whoever compels you to go one mile, go with him two. ⁴²Give to him who asks you, and from him who wants to borrow from you do not turn away. ⁴³You have heard that it was said, 'You shall love your neighbor and hate your enemy.'⁴⁴But I say to you, love your enemies, bless those who curse you, do good to those who hate you, and pray for those who spitefully use you and persecute you, ⁴⁵that you may be sons of your Father in heaven; for He makes His sun rise on the evil and on the good, and sends rain on the just and on the unjust. ⁴⁶For if you love those who love you, what reward have you? Do not even the tax collectors do the same? ⁴⁷And if you greet your brethren only, what do you do more than others? Do not even the tax collectors do so? ⁴⁸Therefore you shall be perfect, just as your Father in heaven is perfect. **Matthew 6:1** Take heed that you do not do your charitable deeds before men, to be seen by them. Otherwise you have no reward from your Father in heaven. ²Therefore, when you do a charitable deed, do not sound a trumpet before you as the hypocrites do in the synagogues and in the streets, that they may have glory from men. Assuredly, I say to you, they have their reward. ³But when you do a charitable deed, do not let your left hand know what your right hand is doing, ⁴that your charitable deed may be in secret; and your Father who sees in secret will Himself reward you openly. ⁵And when you pray, you shall not be like the hypocrites. For they love to pray standing in the synagogues and on the corners of the streets, that they may be seen by men. Assuredly, I say to you, they have their reward. ⁶But you, when you pray, go into your room, and when you have shut your door, pray to your Father who is in the secret place; and your Father who sees in secret will reward you openly. [7]And when you pray, do not use vain repetitions as the heathen do. For they think that they will be heard for their many words. [8]Therefore do not be like them. For your Father knows the things you have need of before you ask Him. [9]In this manner, therefore, pray: Our Father in heaven, Hallowed be Your name. [10]Your kingdom come. Your will be done On earth as it is in heaven. [11]Give us this day our daily bread. [12]And forgive us our debts, As we forgive our debtors. [13]And do not lead us into temptation, But deliver us from the evil one. For Yours is the kingdom and the power and the glory forever. Amen. [14]For if you forgive men their trespasses, your heavenly Father will also forgive you. [15]But if you do not forgive men their trespasses, neither will your Father forgive your trespasses. [16]Moreover, when you fast, do not be like the hypocrites, with a sad countenance. For they disfigure their faces that they may appear to men to be fasting. Assuredly, I say to you, they have their reward. [17]But you, when you fast, anoint your head and wash your face, [18]so that you do not appear to men to be fasting, but to your Father who is in the secret place; and your Father who sees in secret will reward you openly. [19]Do not lay up for yourselves treasures on earth, where moth and rust destroy and where thieves break in and steal; [20]but lay up for yourselves treasures in heaven, where neither moth nor rust destroys and where thieves do not break in and steal. [21]For where your treasure is, there your heart will be also. [22]The lamp of the body is the eye. If therefore your eye is good, your whole body will be full of light. [23]But if your eye is bad, your whole body will be full of darkness. If therefore the light that is in you is darkness, how great is that darkness! [24]No one can serve two masters; for either he will hate the one and love the other, or else he will be loyal to the one and despise the other. You cannot serve God and mammon. [25]Therefore I say to you, do not worry about your life, what you will eat or what you will drink; nor about your body, what you will put on. Is not life more than food and the body more than clothing? [26]Look at the birds of the air, for they neither sow nor reap nor gather into barns; yet your heavenly Father feeds them. Are you not of more value than they? [27]Which of you by worrying can add one cubit to his stature? [28]So why do you worry about clothing? Consider the lilies of the field, how they grow: they neither toil nor spin; [29]and yet I say to you that even Solomon in all his glory was not arrayed like one of these. [30]Now if God so clothes the grass of the field, which today is, and tomorrow is thrown into the oven, will He not much more clothe you, O you of little faith? [31]Therefore do not worry, saying, 'What shall we eat?' or 'What shall we drink?' or 'What shall we wear?' [32]For after all these things the Gentiles seek. For your heavenly Father knows that you need all these things. [33]But seek first the kingdom of God and His righteousness, and all these things shall be added to you. [34]Therefore do not worry about tomorrow, for tomorrow will worry about its own things. Sufficient for the day is its own trouble. **Matthew 7:1** Judge not, that you be not judged. [2]For with what judgment you judge, you will be judged; and with the measure you use, it will be measured back to you. [3]And why do you look at the speck in your brother's eye, but do not consider the plank in your own eye? ⁴Or how can you say to your brother, 'Let me remove the speck from your eye;' and look, a plank is in your own eye? ⁵ Hypocrite! First remove the plank from your own eye, and then you will see clearly to remove the speck from your brother's eye. ⁶Do not give what is holy to the dogs; nor cast your pearls before swine, lest they trample them under their feet, and turn and tear you in pieces. ⁷Ask, and it will be given to you; seek, and you will find; knock, and it will be opened to you. ⁸For everyone who asks receives, and he who seeks finds, and to him who knocks it will be opened. ⁹Or what man is there among you who, if his son asks for bread, will give him a stone? ¹⁰Or if he asks for a fish, will he give him a serpent? ¹¹If you then, being evil, know how to give good gifts to your children, how much more will your Father who is in heaven give good things to those who ask Him! ¹²Therefore, whatever you want men to do to you, do also to them, for this is the Law and the Prophets. ¹³Enter by the narrow gate; for wide is the gate and broad is the way that leads to destruction, and there are many who go in by it. ¹⁴Because narrow is the gate and difficult is the way which leads to life, and there are few who find it. ¹⁵Beware of false prophets, who come to you in sheep's clothing, but inwardly they are ravenous wolves. ¹⁶You will know them by their fruits. Do men gather grapes from thornbushes or figs from thistles? ¹⁷Even so, every good tree bears good fruit, but a bad tree bears bad fruit. ¹⁸A good tree cannot bear bad fruit, nor can a bad tree bear good fruit. ¹⁹Every tree that does not bear good fruit is cut down and thrown into the fire. ²⁰Therefore by their fruits you will know them. ²¹Not everyone who says to Me, 'Lord, Lord,' shall enter the kingdom of heaven, but he who does the will of My Father in heaven. ²²Many will say to Me in that day, 'Lord, Lord, have we not prophesied in Your name, cast out demons in Your name, and done many wonders in Your name?' ²³And then I will declare to them, 'I never knew you; depart from Me, you who practice lawlessness!' ²⁴Therefore whoever hears these sayings of Mine, and does them, I will liken him to a wise man who built his house on the rock: ²⁵and the rain descended, the floods came, and the winds blew and beat on that house; and it did not fall, for it was founded on the rock. ²⁶But everyone who hears these sayings of Mine, and does not do them, will be like a foolish man who built his house on the sand: ²⁷ and the rain descended, the floods came, and the winds blew and beat on that house; and it fell. And great was its fall. ²⁸And so it was, when Jesus had ended these sayings, that the people were astonished at His teaching, ²⁹for He taught them as one having authority, and not as the scribes. ᴺᴷᴶ

What was most familiar to you?


What was most surprising to you?

*Oh! Wow! That was my response when I saw how often the kingdom of heaven was referred to in this sermon. It is mentioned clearly at the beginning and the end, and is referred to in one way or another throughout its entirety.*

How did Matthew prepare us to hear this sermon? What did he bring attention to in Matthew 4:17 and Matthew 4:23? What did he say that Jesus preached?

---

…The King's first proclamation was of good news, God's marvelous offer to deliver "us from the domain of darkness, and [to transfer] us to the kingdom of His beloved Son, in whom we have redemption, the forgiveness of sins" (Col. 1:13-14). The gospel is the good news of salvation through Jesus Christ, the good news that God's kingdom (the sphere of God's rule by the grace of salvation) is open to anyone who puts his trust in the King.[11]

---

*Jesus' message is all about the Kingdom of Heaven and John MacArthur calls it a homiletical masterpiece. He gives the following outline:*

    *I.     Matthew 5:1 – 12: Introduction – the possibility of happiness*

    *II.    Matthew 5:13 – 16: Citizens of the Kingdom*

    *III.   Matthew 5:17 – 7:12: Righteousness of the Kingdom*

    *IV.   Matthew 7:13 – 29: Exhortation to enter the Kingdom*

    *V.    Matthew 7::28 – 29: Conclusion – the effect of the sermon on the hearers* [12]

Please mark these sections in your copy of the Sermon in your workbook.

*Realizing that the Sermon on the Mount relates to how to live in the realm of the Messiah's kingdom will impact how we apply these Scriptures to our lives. Christians over the years have proposed several perspectives on how to interpret and apply this message. A few of them, briefly summarized, are: 1) that the sermon was for the Jews of Jesus day and how they should live at that time, 2) that the sermon presented moral standards for the church during Matthew's time, and 3) that the sermon is the law for the Millennial Kingdom.*

*Most of the commentaries that I have used explain these different viewpoints, and give the reasons that they are not based on a full, literal interpretation of the Scriptures. I'd like to share with you once again from MacArthur's commentary because his summary is so clear and thorough. This will set the stage for how we will interpret the Sermon as well as the rest of the book of Matthew.*

Because of its seemingly impossible demands, many evangelicals maintain that the Sermon on the Mount pertains only to the kingdom age, the Millennium. (The Millennial Kingdom is defined as Jesus' thousand year reign on earth after the Tribulation and Armageddon.) Otherwise, they argue, how could Jesus command us to be perfect, just as our "heavenly Father is perfect" (Matt.5:48)?

For several reasons, however, that interpretation cannot be correct.

1st - the text does not indicate or imply that these teachings are for another age.

2nd - Jesus demanded them of people who were not living in the Millennium.

3rd - many of the teachings themselves become meaningless if they are applied to the Millennium. For example, there will be no persecution of believers (see Matt. 5:10-12, 44) during the kingdom age.

4th - every principle taught in the Sermon on the Mount is also taught elsewhere in the New Testament in contexts that clearly apply to believers of our present age.

5th - there are many New Testament passages that command equally impossible standards, which unglorified human strength cannot continually achieve (see Rom. 13:14; 2 Cor. 7:1; Phil 1:9-10; Col. 3:1-2; Heb. 12:14; 1 Pet. 1:15-16).

The teachings of the Sermon on the Mount are for believers today, marking the distinctive life-style that should characterize the direction, if not the perfection, of the lives of Christians of every age.[13]

*Today has been a time of preparation for our upcoming study on Matthew 5-7. We needed this overview before looking at the specifics of this amazing message. I needed it so that I could become prepared to take this great message to heart. I've already begun to be challenged. But I know that because I have trusted in Jesus as my Savior and King, He has given me the new life that I need to be able to follow His teaching. Only through the power of the Holy Spirit can I live as a citizen of the kingdom of heaven. There is no better place to call home!*

*Even though we've already heard the whole sermon, let's go back to the very beginning and get situated on the mountain with Jesus and His disciples to see how it all started.*

What characterized the multitudes that Jesus saw, according to Matthew 4:24-5:1? And what was Jesus' purpose in speaking to them, according to Matthew 5:2?

What was the response of the people at the end of His message, according to Matthew 7:28-29?

Do you recognize the authority with which Jesus speaks? Are you amazed or inspired by His teaching? What are your initial responses to His teaching in the Sermon on the Mount?

# Unit Two   Matthew 5:1 — 48

# JESUS' BLESSINGS

*For years teachers and preachers have been trained to begin their lessons with something that will intrigue their students, something that will draw them in and whet their appetites for the message that is to be explained. Interesting stories, humorous anecdotes, surprising statements, intriguing questions – these are all used to captivate the audience and lead them into the main points of the message. It's called "the hook."*

*Jesus just called some fishermen to become fishers of men and He Himself goes fishing with a hook baited with the most wonderful new way of life. There is no "bait and switch," no trick up His sleeve – just the truth about the characteristics and blessings of one who is a citizen of the kingdom of heaven. But it is shocking! Let's look at His opening comments on life in the kingdom, known to us as the Beatitudes.*

Ask the Holy Spirit to enable you to rejoice in the blessings you receive in Christ.

**Please read Matthew 5:1-16.** These are the nine Beatitudes (vs.3-12), plus two more descriptions of the citizens of the kingdom of heaven. (You'll note them in the blanks below.)

Please look up the definition for the following word:

**Blessed: Strong's #3107**

**Greek word:**

**Greek definition:**

*I've often heard that happiness is a superficial emotion, and joy on the other hand is the deeper sense of delight, satisfaction, and well-being. But Jesus is certainly not talking about a superficial happiness.*

*Why does Jesus say that the people He describes are happy? Each of the Beatitudes contains a special word in Greek, which we have translated as "for," which means "because, since, for this reason," and it is used to explain the basis for the happiness being declared.*

Fill in the blanks below as we consider what you can experience when you follow Jesus as your Savior and King. Just note the phrase following "for." We'll return to the characteristics later.

**Matthew 5:3:** Blessed (happy), because: _____

**Matthew 5:4:** Blessed (happy), because: _____

**Matthew 5:5:** Blessed (happy), because: _____

**Matthew 5:6:** Blessed (happy), because: _____

**Matthew 5:7:** Blessed (happy), because: _____

**Matthew 5:8**: Blessed (happy), because: _____

**Matthew 5:9:** Blessed (happy), because: _____

**Matthew 5:10:** Blessed (happy), because: _____

**Matthew 5:11-12:** Blessed (happy), because: _____

How would you describe the emotional and spiritual state of one who is experiencing all of the above? Use a thesaurus if you need to do so!

> The word *makarios* describes the nearly incomprehensible happiness of those who participate in the kingdom announced by Jesus. Rather than happiness in its mundane sense, it refers to the deep inner joy of those who have long awaited the salvation promised by God and who now begin to experience its fulfillment. The *makarioi* are the deeply or supremely happy.[14]

*This is the good news of the gospel! True, wonderful, deep, satisfying happiness is possible. If — if we are the people described in these verses. Some people see the Beatitudes as the road to salvation. But, Ephesians 2:8-9 says that we are saved by grace, not by works. If we tried to produce the characteristics described in the Beatitudes, we'd be working in our own strength to achieve salvation. So, these statements describe the characteristics and behaviors of one who has received new life in Christ and is filled with a new nature, empowered by the Holy Spirit and therefore able to live as described.*

How do the Beatitudes describe one who is following Jesus as her Savior and King? You don't have to explain each characteristic, just make a list from Matthew 5:3-12. (For example: verse 3: poor in spirit)

*The first four characteristics pertain to our relationship with God, and the next five pertain to our relationship with man.[15] We will take time to look at each of the statements one by one over the next several lessons.*

Blessed are the poor in spirit, for theirs is the kingdom of heaven. Matthew 5:3 [NAS]

Please look up the definition for the following word:
**Poor: Strong's #4434**
**Greek word:**
**Greek definition:**

The same word is used in Isaiah 61:1, and Jesus said in Luke 4:18-21 that He Himself fulfilled this Scripture. Please record what is declared in these verses.

Please look up the definition of the following word in the Hebrew:

**Poor: Strong's #6035**

**Hebrew word:**

**Hebrew definition:**

What is requested in Psalm 40:17 where this same word is used?

And what is promised in James 2:5?

Based on the Greek and Hebrew definitions, and the verses above, how would you explain the phrase: "poor in spirit"?

*This phrase is found nowhere else in the Bible, but it is used in the Dead Sea Scrolls to describe the members of the Qumran community whose members took a vow of poverty in dependence upon God for righteousness and sustenance.[16] In Matthew, it describes the condition of those who are absolutely destitute no matter what their financial, social, educational or religious status, and they are therefore completely reliant on God in every way for every need.*

Are you among the poor in spirit? How would you describe this in your own life?

*Please note the incredible paradox that Jesus presents. Being poor in spirit does not mean being depressed! Recognizing the depravity of our condition and our helplessness without the help of Christ leads to the ultimate gain of heaven and the greatest happiness!*

# JESUS' PARADOXES

*The next Beatitude presents another paradox: happy are the sad. Hmmm. Does that mean that we are happy and sad at the same time? Let's look at the timing in this verse.*

> Pray that the Holy Spirit, the Comforter, will give you His perspective as you study.

Blessed are those who mourn, for they shall be comforted. Matthew 5:4 <sup>NAS</sup>
Why is there mourning? Look at the context in Matthew 5:3-12 for situations that would cause grief.

When does the blessedness happen? When does the mourning happen? When does the comforting happen?

*While there is mourning at the present, there is a promise of comfort in the future. The first and last Beatitudes are in present tense in the Greek, which shows us that the poor in spirit and the persecuted don't have to wait until a future time to belong to the kingdom of heaven. But the 2<sup>nd</sup> through 7<sup>th</sup> Beatitudes each use future tense, and this shows us that we don't receive everything related to the kingdom of heaven yet. This is an "already and not yet" perspective. The kingdom of heaven is at hand, and is still yet to come and to be realized in its entirety.*

How will we be comforted in the future? Note the promises from the following verses:

**Isaiah 25:8**

**John 16:22**

**Romans 8:18**

**Revelation 21:4**

From whom does this comfort come? How does Matthew 5:4 communicate that? (Hint: look at the way the verb is written.)

While being comforted is a blessing from our relationship with the Lord, it is also something to be shared. What does 2 Corinthians 1:3-4 tell us?

So, what do you think? Does Matthew 5:4 mean that Christians are happy and sad at the same time during our lives here on earth right now? Please explain your answer.

*The next characteristic of the citizen of heaven is found in Matthew 5:5: Blessed are the meek for they shall inherit the earth. This is another paradox. It is a surprising statement, especially for those sitting under the dominion of the Roman Empire. Brute strength and powerful oppression ruled the vast regions of the Caesars, as well as the Judean territories under King Herod. The meek would inherit the earth? Not if Herod and Augustus had anything to say about it.*

Please look up the following word:
**Meek: Strong's #4239**
**Greek word:**
**Greek definition:**

The best way to come to an understanding of this Beatitude is to look at its source. Please read Psalm 37:7-11.

What is the problem in these verses?

What is the instruction?

What is the promise?

*This promise of inheriting the earth goes back to God's promise to Abraham found in Genesis 13:15: "I will give all the land that you see to you and your descendants forever."* [NET] *Those who are oppressed by the unjust rulers of the world, who are humbly waiting on the Lord and His timing, will one day enjoy complete, perfect peace on earth under the rule of the King of Justice.*

How do the meek behave, based on the definition and verses above?

*Knowing the authority and holiness of God is what will lead us to walk in meekness. Our righteous, sovereign Lord has everything under control, and we can trust Him.*

Paul encourages us to live with the gentleness of this Beatitude in the following verses. What do they say, and how does this mean that you should respond to the authorities in your community and government today?

**1 Timothy 2:1-3**

**Romans 13:1**

*Now let's look at the fourth Beatitude.*

Blessed are those who hunger and thirst for righteousness, for they shall be filled.

Matthew 5:6 [KJV]

What happens to you when you are extremely hungry or thirsty?

*This Beatitude is different from the others, because it tells you what you should want, as well as telling you what you will receive. Its placement in the middle of the Beatitudes highlights righteousness, and we will see through the rest of the Sermon on the Mount that this is the central, all-encompassing characteristic of the citizens of the kingdom of heaven.*

What is righteousness? Look back at page 20 and summarize the meaning of this word.

> In Matthew, "righteousness" speaks of right behavior before God. Protestant Christians who are used to reading Paul may think that Matthew is speaking of the imputed righteousness of Christ (cf. ., Rom. 5:1-2), but this…is not a Matthean nuance. Here the emphasis is on the practical side, the upright lifestyle. [17]

Note what the following verses from the Sermon on the Mount say about righteousness:

**Matthew 5:10**

**Matthew 5:20**

**Matthew 6:1**

**Matthew 6:33**

*We will look at the attitudes and actions of those who are pursuing righteousness through the rest of the Sermon on the Mount, as well as throughout the book of Matthew. This concept of the pursuit of righteousness is repeated throughout his gospel.*

When you are hungry and thirsty and your physical needs are satisfied, does that mean that you'll never be hungry or thirsty again? How does this relate to longing for righteousness?

*Keep in mind that the Beatitudes describe the characteristics and behaviors of one who is following Jesus Christ. Our study so far has made me realize that I need to pray for the Lord to continue to bring about these attitudes in my life. We will look at the rest of the Beatitudes in our next lesson. Please conclude today in prayer, asking the Lord to transform you into one who is poor in spirit, mourning, meek, and yearning for righteousness, so that you will experience the blessedness of the kingdom of heaven!*

---

Lesson Three: Matthew 5:5-16

# JESUS' EXPECTATIONS

*Welcome to the Beatitudes, part two! Remember that we are still in the surprising introduction to the Sermon on the Mount. What Jesus is saying is enticing, but it is also as strange to our ears as it was to those of His own day. How does someone live the way that is being described? The characteristics of those who belong in the kingdom of heaven can only come from the supernatural power of the Holy Spirit. We must have a new nature so that we can live in a new way.*

Summarize what you learn from Ephesians 4:17-24.

*Put on the new nature! And it will look just like those who are described in the Beatitudes! If we have trusted in Jesus as our Savior, we have received the Holy Spirit; and we are therefore new creations. Our lifestyles and longings will be different than they were before. Based on what we saw in the last lesson, we will be "poor in spirit" – humble and dependent. We will "mourn" – over sin, depravity, suffering. We will be "meek" – humble and submissive to God's authority in our lives. We will "hunger and thirst after righteousness" – this will be the desire that consumes us and nothing less than pleasing God will satisfy us. And we will be "merciful," "pure in heart," and "peacemakers." Let's learn about these characteristics today.*

Blessed are the merciful, for they shall obtain mercy. Matthew 5:7 KJV

God Himself is merciful and we are to be like Him.    Himself. Please note how God demonstrates His mercy in the following verses:

**Exodus 34:6**


**Nehemiah 9:16-17**


**Jeremiah 3:12**


How did Jesus demonstrate mercy according to the following verses?

**Matthew 9:35-37**


**Matthew 20:29-34**


**Hebrews 2:17**

Based on the demonstrations of mercy shown by God the Father and Jesus His Son, how then should we demonstrate mercy to others?

*Another God-like characteristic shows up in the next Beatitude:*

Blessed are the pure in heart, for they shall see God. Matthew 5:8 <sup>KJV</sup>

Please look up the definition for the following word:

**Pure: Strong's #2513**
**Greek word:**
**Greek definition:**

How does Psalm 24:3-5 explain the importance of being pure in heart?

*Of all the descriptions of a citizen of the kingdom of heaven, this one is the most challenging. Without a new nature, you might be able to come pretty close to living out every other characteristic; but there is no way to clean up your heart.*

**According to Ezekiel 36:25-29:**

Who changes your heart?

How?

Why?

How does Hebrews 10:19-22 explain this cleansing and what is the result? How does this relate to the Beatitude and the Psalm?

*Does the promise of seeing God surprise you? Confuse you? Exodus 33:20 says that no man can see the face of God and live. But there is a "new and living way" to enter God's presence and see Him. Right now, we see Him with eyes of faith; and in the future, it will be face to face! This is the greatest possible reward, obtained only through the grace and mercy of the Lord.*

How do the following verses confirm this hope?

**1 John 3:2-3**

**Revelation 21:22-22:4**

*Wow! One day. I hope it's soon! Meanwhile, I'll live so others can see Him in me.*

Blessed are the peacemakers, for they shall be called sons of God. Matthew 5:9 [NAS]

As the Lord has done to us, so should we do to others. What do the following verses tell you about making peace?

**Isaiah 52:7**

**Romans 5:1-2**

**2 Corinthians 13:11**

**Hebrews 12:14**

| This beatitude is not about being a passively peaceful person but about being an active reconciler of people... Jesus's disciples actively seek harmonious relationships with others. [18] |
| --- |

Is this beatitude evident in your life? Are you a peacemaker? How?

*If we share the peace of God with others and seek peace with them, then we will all be one big happy family, right? Only if they make peace with God themselves. Those who are not reconciled to God will very likely be antagonistic in some way towards us. And that leads us to the last two Beatitudes. Take a break and we'll study them in the next lesson.*

Lesson Four: Matthew 5:10-20

# JESUS' CITIZENS

*No need for an introduction. Just remember how we ended the last lesson. Those not reconciled to God will very likely be antagonistic in some way toward us.*

> Be joyful always; pray continually; give thanks in
> all circumstances, for this is God's will for you.
> 1 Thessalonians 5:16-18 [NIV]

**Please read Matthew 5:10-12.**

How are the citizens of the kingdom of heaven treated?

Why are they treated this way?

How are they to react to these circumstances?

*We have another extreme paradox. In the midst of the pain of persecution, we are to be happy – that wonderful, deep, satisfying blessedness. Because the hope of the future is greater than the hurt of today.*

How might you experience persecution today?

And how should you respond, based on all the Beatitudes?

*It is this life of righteousness that will stand out in the darkness of the world and point others to Heaven. This is what Jesus explains in the last few sentences of His introduction to the Sermon on the Mount.*

**Please read Matthew 5:13-16.**

*These are probably very familiar verses. The two metaphors of salt and light would have been easily understood by Jesus' disciples and the rest of the crowd that gathered around Him. Salt was a valuable substance with many uses: seasoning, preserving, purifying, and fertilizing. Light is important for almost all activity and even more critical in the dark to keep one from stumbling.*

Jesus makes surprising comments about both salt and light. What unlikely scenarios does He describe?

*Did you know that real salt – the compound sodium chloride (NaCl) – is stable and cannot lose its flavor? It doesn't change. But, there was another substance consisting of salt and gypsum that was collected from the Dead Sea by evaporation.[19] It was not pure salt, and it was not good for seasoning or preserving and was considered useless.*

*And how useless would a lamp be, hidden under a basket? "The lamp used in a typical Palestinian home was a partially closed reservoir made of clay. It had a hole on top to pour oil in and a spout on one end into which a wick of flax or cotton was set. It was a fairly small lamp, which gave off only a modest light; thus, to give maximum illumination it was placed on a lampstand."[20] The only time that it made sense to cover the lamp would be when they wanted to extinguish the light.*

*These two metaphors and their improbabilities highlight the same unlikely situations in the lives of disciples. A true disciple, a real follower of Jesus Christ with a changed life, will never lose her saltiness and will never hide the light of Christ from the world. Only those who do not truly know Him as their Savior will become useless.*

How and why are you to let your light shine, according to Matthew 5:14-16?

*True disciples of Christ demonstrating the characteristics of the Beatitudes will show their saltiness and their light will shine.*

How can the world around you notice that you are:

Poor in spirit?

Mourning over sin and suffering?

Meek?

Hungering and thirsting for righteousness?

Merciful?

Pure in heart?

A peacemaker?


Persecuted for righteousness sake?


*We've completed our first study of Jesus' words — words in red letters. These are from the heart of Jesus, to you and me. How precious they are and how practical they are! We have heard in the Beatitudes of the greatest life possible – life in the kingdom that belongs to the King of Kings. It's a life of righteousness that we can only live by the power of the Holy Spirit. And that was just the introduction! We have a lot to learn ahead of us. But there is no better Teacher than Jesus Himself. Praise Him that He came to earth, to speak to you.*

*Jesus has a few more words of introduction to give us before He launches into the main message of His most famous sermon of all time. You'll see in the next verses that righteousness – that is – right living which pleases God – is the key to entering the Kingdom of Heaven.*

**Please read Matthew 5:17-20.**

*What are "the Law and the Prophets"? Let's look at a few other verses from the New Testament that will help us understand these code words.*

What do you learn about the Law and the Prophets from the following verses?

**Luke 24:44**


**John 1:45**


**Acts 13:15**


**Romans 3:21**


Based on Matthew 5:17-20, what will not happen?


And based on the same passage as above, what will happen?

*Jesus was preaching to the poor, the peasants, and the common people, and He told them they had to be more righteous than the most religious people they knew – the scribes and Pharisees! His statement must have bewildered his audience.*

*Highlight the phrases and concepts that refer to the "righteousness" of the scribes and Pharisees in the commentary below. You'll see that it was more about rules and regulations than rightly responding to God.*

---

While it was the aim of Jesus to call men to the law of God itself as the supreme guide of life, the Pharisees, upon the pretense of maintaining it intact, multiplied minute precepts and distinctions, to such an extent that the whole life of the Israelite was hemmed in, and burdened on every side, by instructions so numerous and trifling, that the law was almost if not wholly lost sight of. These "traditions" as they were called, had long been gradually accumulating.

Of the trifling character of these regulations, innumerable instances are to be found in the Mishnah. Such were their washings before they could eat bread, and the special minuteness with which the forms of this washing were prescribed; their bathing when they returned from the market; their washing of cups, pots, brazen vessels, etc.; their fastings twice in the week, (Luke. 18:12), as were their tithing; (Mat. 23:23), and such, finally, were those minute and vexatious extensions of the law of the Sabbath, which must have converted God's gracious ordinance of the Sabbath's rest, into a burden and a pain. (Mat.12:1-13.) [21]

---

Based on your highlighting, how would you describe the righteousness of the Sadducees and Pharisees?



*What a relief Jesus' words will be. He won't be adding more rules to the Pharisees list. Instead, He'll show how righteousness comes from within and overflows from the heart. Remember – this sermon shows how a member of the kingdom of heaven lives, and this lifestyle is only possible by the power of the indwelling Holy Spirit.*

---

Lesson Five: Matthew 5:21-44

## JESUS SAYS DON'T

*Let the main message begin! Let's take a look at Jesus' radical repeated statements. Six times He says, "you have heard that it was said…… but I say to you…." It's a good thing He already told us that He had not come to destroy the Law and the Prophets! His listeners could have gotten the wrong idea!*

Pause and pray for the understanding
of what Jesus says and why He says it.

In Matthew 5:21-44, what were the traditional sayings and what did Jesus say? Fill in the chart on the next page..

| "You have heard that it was said…" | "But I say to you…" |
| --- | --- |
| 5:21 | 5:22 |
| 5:27 | 5:28 |
| 5:31 | 5:32 |
| 5:33 | 5:37 |
| 5:38 | 5:39 |
| 5:43 | 5:44 |

*Each of the old sayings were based on clear commandments given by the Lord. The books of Exodus, Leviticus, Numbers and Deuteronomy recorded the lifestyle that God intended for His people. But the rabbis, Pharisees, Sadducees, and scribes had added their own traditions to the truth.*

*Jesus didn't contradict God's Words, but He did contradict what the people got wrong. In the Greek, word order is often important, and pronouns are often not necessary. In these verses, however, we have the pronoun "I" coming first in the sentence, so Jesus was emphasizing His words as being the ultimate authoritative words to live by.*

**Please read Matthew 5:21-26.**

What two scenarios have the same outcome in verses 21-22?

What are the consequences of the other two scenarios in verse 22?

Do you think the severity of the sin is equal to the severity of the consequence? What do these scenarios teach you about your internal attitudes?

---

"The fire of hell" (NIV), "fiery hell" (NAS), "hell fire" (NKJ) are the phrases used to express what is literally "the Gehenna of fire" in the Greek. Gehenna, or the Valley of Hinnom as it was also called, was a place outside of Jerusalem where human sacrifices had been offered to the god Molech at one time in Israel's history. It eventually became a garbage dump for the city where fire continually burned. Because of the constant fire, Gehenna became an appropriate symbol for eternal punishment. [22]

---

Jesus doesn't just say "don't be angry," He explains what to do when you do get angry or discover that others are angry with you. What actions does He describe and what are the motivations for those actions?

*I wasn't angry with anyone...until I read this passage and started studying it! Then a little conversation got a little frustrating. And before you know it, I got angry! But the Holy Spirit convicted me quickly and reconciliation followed.*

So, now, how about you? How's your temper? Who pushes your buttons? Is there anyone you need to go to and be reconciled with?

*"Whoever says, 'You fool!' shall be in danger of hell fire." Wow! That's something they had never heard before! The laws of God were not just about external actions – they were about internal attitudes as well. And before they could catch their breath in amazement, Jesus continued with more teaching..."you have heard that it was said...."*

**Read Matthew 5:27-30.**

What's the complete definition for adultery based on Jesus' explanation?

*And once again, Jesus doesn't just say: "Don't do it." With eloquent and deliberate exaggeration, Jesus describes the extreme action that must be taken when faced with temptation.*

But if you pluck out one eye, and cut off one hand, can you still commit adultery? (Explain!)

*This brief passage about adultery doesn't actually tell you how to keep from committing adultery does it? Jesus is explaining that our thoughts are as critical as our actions. This is just one of His examples as He teaches that only those whose "righteousness exceeds that of the Pharisees" can enter the Kingdom of Heaven.*

*The teachings from the Sermon on the Mount prompt us to say – "how can I live that way?" We can't, in our own strength. It's only by the power of the Holy Spirit. (I've mentioned that before, haven't I? And I'm sure that I'll share it again.)*

What is Jesus' next example of true righteousness about? See Matthew 5:31-32.

*This is not the only time that Jesus will teach about adultery, marriage, and divorce. He has more to say about it in Matthew 19, so we will spend more time on these topics in later lessons.*

"Again, you have heard…" What was the problem in Matthew 5:33-36?


What do Leviticus 19:12 and Deuteronomy 23:23 teach?


How did Jesus say righteousness would be demonstrated, according to Matthew 5:37?


Take a moment to check your own vocabulary. Do you say what you mean and mean what you say? How would you describe the way that you communicate? Do you need to make any changes?


Look back over the chart at the beginning of this lesson and your notes. What is on our "don't" list? Summarize the righteous behaviors that characterize our lives as members of the kingdom of heaven.


*We aren't finished with Jesus' illustrations of true righteousness. We'll pick up in the middle of this passage in our next lesson. We will want to spend some time on the next two statements!*

---

 Lesson Six: Matthew 5:38-48

# JESUS SAYS DO

*"You have heard that it was said, 'An eye for an eye, and a tooth for a tooth.' But I say to you…" Matthew 5:38* [NKJ] *Here it comes… that incredible teaching that is so difficult for us to live by.*

> Pray that the Holy Spirit will lead
> you to obey the word of God.

What does Jesus say in Matthew 5:39-42?


*This is true righteousness. Hmmm. How so? Righteousness – right living – is a reflection of who God is. Jesus demonstrated it. So this is to be demonstrated in our lives too. God certainly turned the other cheek again and again with the Israelites.*

*If we demand that justice must be served and we take matters into our own hands to avenge the wrongs done to us, then we are forgetting the grace that was shown to us. When Jesus was beaten, cursed, and crucified, He did not retaliate. When we were enemies of God, He extended kindness to us.*

*We were saved, not by justice, not by vengeance, but by grace. As members of the kingdom of heaven, we are to give to others that same grace which we have received.*

The following verses teach us this concept. How do they say it?

**Romans 12:17-21**


**1 Thessalonians 5:15**


**1 Peter 3:9**


*But what about justice? What about retaliation? When will the wicked get what they deserve?*

You just read the verse that settles the issue. Look back at your notes from Romans 12:19 and note how the wicked will receive what they deserve.



*Citizens of the kingdom of heaven will trust God to carry out the justice required in His way at His time.*

*The last example of true righteousness is very closely related to the one we just looked at.*

**Please read Matthew 5:43-48.**

What actually was said in Leviticus 19:18 which was referenced in Matthew 5:43?

"You shall hate your enemy," though not taught in the Old Testament, is an inference that was commonly drawn, for example, from such passages as Psalm 139:21-22; 26:5; or Deuteronomy 7:2; 30:7. On the basis of such passages, the Qumranites explicitly taught hatred of those regarded as enemies. Clearly, neither Jesus' listeners nor Matthew's readers would have been surprised by the added words, since the traditional interpretation had become regularly associated with the text. The "neighbor" meant fellow Jew; the "enemy" meant Gentile. [23]

But Jesus said love your enemies! How? What specific actions does Jesus tell us to take in Matthew 5:44?

Who are your enemies?

Why are we to love our enemies and pray for those who persecute us, according to Matthew 5:45-48?

*One of Jesus' disciples, who had been quick to assault Jesus' enemy, eventually learned the lesson from the Sermon on the Mount. He wrote to Christians who were being persecuted and reminded them of Jesus' teaching. Peter, the disciple who cut off a soldier's ear, learned how to live as a citizen of the Kingdom of Heaven.*

In 1 Peter 3:13-18, what does Peter say that parallels Matthew 5:44-48?

I asked you earlier who your enemies are. Now it's time for the question: how have you treated your enemies? Do you need to make any changes?

*Love our enemies! Suffer for doing good! That's just what Jesus did – for us – who were once His enemies. This is the golden rule with a twist. Do unto others as you have been done unto. This is how we are to live. Jesus' instructions to us are not a list of rules: they are a description of the attitude of the heart. It doesn't come naturally, but it does come supernaturally.*

Please read through the first portion of the Sermon again: **Matthew 5:1-48** (page 28-29).

All of these actions in Matthew 5:21-48 are in regards to what? (Please don't skip this question! Make a note of your thoughts.)

**Which of the following areas apply to the teaching in each topic below?**

1. My relationship with God

2. My own life

3. My relationship with the others

4. My relationship with the church

Matthew 5:21-26: Anger _____     Matthew 5:33-37: Communication _____

Matthew 5:27-30: Adultery _____     Matthew 5:38-42: Revenge _____

Matthew 5:31-32: Divorce _____     Matthew 5:43-48: Enemies _____

What has been the most interesting, revealing, or convicting aspect of our lessons on these topics?

*Do you remember what Jesus said before He explained the warped teachings of the Pharisees? He said that unless your righteousness exceeds that of the Pharisees, you will not enter the Kingdom of Heaven. We've just looked at His first real-life examples of what righteousness looks like. Our relationships with others will reflect our relationship with our Lord.*

*More tangible, practical teaching is on the way. Stay tuned!*

# Unit Three  Matthew 6:1 — 7:29

Lesson One: Matthew 6:1-18

# JESUS KNOWS OUR SECRETS

*If I had been listening to Jesus' Sermon on the Mount, I think I would have been very convicted by His words so far. I would have been thinking: "My behavior has to be better than that of the Pharisees? I can't just look good on the outside? My thoughts and attitudes have to be righteous, loving, and perfect, too?" I don't know about you, but when I get convicted, I start looking for ways to rationalize that I'm really not that bad. "But I go to church. And I give to charities. And I pray for missionaries."*

*Those good deeds must also be examined. And that's just what Jesus talks about next. Even our righteous actions must be done with the proper motivation and presentation.*

> Ask the Spirit of God to strengthen you in your inner being where He alone knows your thoughts.

*I'd like for you to get an overview of the next section of the sermon. Jesus has a three point outline and makes an impact with repetition.*

**Please read Matthew 6:1-18.**

Look at the following outline and fill in the blanks.

I.  **Matthew 6:1** - Introductory statement: "Take heed that you do not do your

_____, to be seen by them. Otherwise, you have

_____ .

II.  **Matthew 6:2** - First righteous act: "When you _____,

do not _____. Truly I say to you, _____.

III.  **Matthew 6:5** – Second righteous act: "When you _____,

do not _____. Truly I say to you, _____.

IV.  **Matthew 6:16** – Third righteous act: "When you _____,

do not _____. Truly I say to you, _____.

*Even good deeds can be carried out for the wrong reasons. If we are giving, praying, and fasting so that others will see us and applaud our spirituality, then we will receive no applause from Heaven for those actions.*

*Our good works done for man's approval will not give us God's approval. But good works – righteous actions – are the expected result of our relationship with God the Father and Jesus His Son; and that's what Jesus is teaching about.*

What does Ephesians 2:10 say?

And how does Jesus tell us to do some of those good works? Once again, fill in the blanks below. We are still looking at Jesus' three-point outline and His use of repetition!

I.      **Matthew 6:3-4:** First righteous act: But when you give to the needy, _____, so that your giving may be in _____, and your Father who sees in _____ will _____.

II.     **Matthew 6:6:** Second righteous act: But when you pray, _____, and pray to your Father who is in _____, and your Father who sees in _____ will _____.

III.    **Matthew 6:16-18:** Third righteous act: But when you fast, _____, but by your Father who is in _____, and your Father who sees in _____ will _____.

*Filling in the blanks as we read through these verses is relatively easy. It's actually processing these instructions and practicing them in our lives that's challenging. We must learn not to sound the trumpet (don't blow your own horn!) in all areas of spiritual disciplines.*

What does Jesus call those who practice their righteous deeds so that all will see them and applaud them? (Matthew 6:2, 5, 16)


Please look up the definition for the following word:
**Hypocrites: Strong's #5273**
**Greek word:**
**Greek definition:**



How can you keep your left hand from knowing what your right hand is doing when you give?



There are many times when believers pray in public and this is appropriate. What should our perspective be when we pray together in a group?



*Let's consider the practice of fasting now. The next lesson will be devoted to the Lord's Prayer.*

*In each of Jesus' comments regarding the Jews' regular religious activities (giving, praying, and fasting), He refers to them as things that the disciples will continue to do as faithful followers of His. They will still give, and they will still pray, and they will still fast. This is indicated by the word "when" in Matthew 6:3, 7, and 16.*

The Old Testament law required only one fast a year – on the Day of Atonement. How does Leviticus 16:29-30 describe the action the people are to take?

*The fast on the Day of Atonement was to bring people to a place of remorse and repentance regarding their sin. Throughout the course of Israel's history, additional days of fasting became a part of their religious calendar. Some Jews even fasted twice a week, on Mondays and Thursdays, because they believed that Moses climbed up Mount Sinai on those days.*

Who is described in Luke 18:9-12, what did he do, and what was his attitude?

Colossians 2:20-23 also tells us something about abstaining from foods. It says that rules such as "do not handle, do not taste, do not touch" have the appearance of wisdom.

Who made these rules and why do they have the appearance of wisdom?

Are these rules of any value?

How does Jesus say that his disciples should fast in Matthew 6:17-18?

*Anointing the head and washing the face were not special rituals that were to accompany abstaining from food; instead, they were extra measures of grooming and personal hygiene. Jesus' disciples were to look even better when fasting than when they weren't!*

There is one more discussion about fasting that takes place in Matthew 9:14-15. What does Jesus explain about fasting here? (Jesus is the bridegroom! The disciples are His attendants! Make sure that you recognize the word "mourn" as a synonym for "fast".)

Let's sum up what we've discovered about fasting:

**According to the Old Testament –**

The purpose of fasting was:

The manner of fasting was:

**According to Jesus –**

The wrong way to fast was:

The wrong time to fast was:

The right way to fast was:

The right time to fast was:

*There is only one occasion of fasting mentioned in the time of the early church. I'd like you to see that there is an example of corporate fasting.*

What do you learn from Acts 13:1-3?

*I have found in my own life that it is more difficult to fast for the right reasons than to give or pray for the right reason. I don't want to fast to be proud of my spiritual discipline; I don't want to fast to try to manipulate God. I'll admit that I'm usually more motivated to fast when I've had too much to eat! That's the wrong reason as well.*

*This lesson hasn't motivated me to fast. But even if it had, I wouldn't tell you! Whatever your practice of fasting, make sure that it's between you and your Lord.*

To what spiritual activities, rituals, or traditions in our churches today do we need to apply Jesus' teachings?

---

Lesson Two: Matthew 6:5-18

## JESUS TEACHES US TO PRAY

*Oh, what a precious time in prayer we should have today as we learn how to pray from Jesus. There is no better teacher than He! While many pastors would rather refer to His prayer as "the disciple's prayer" or "the model prayer," I'm just going to refer to it as it is most commonly known...the Lord's prayer.*

It's time to pray about prayer! What is your need?

**Please read Matthew 6:5-14.**

I'm going to ask you a personal question, one that I hope you will answer (and share with others if you are in a group). How would you describe your prayers? When do you pray? Where do you pray?

Now let's look at the prayers of the pretenders…the hypocrites…the Pharisees. According to Matthew 6:5-14, what were two problems with their prayers and why were they problems?

Problem #1:

  Because:

Problem #2:

  Because:

Jesus says: "Do not be like them." Why? What does He explain in Matthew 6:6 and 8?

*After explaining what not to do and why not to do it, Jesus tells the disciples – "in this manner, therefore… pray." One little Greek word —"outos" — is used to point the disciples in the right direction. This word which can be translated as "in this way," "in this manner," "likewise," and "in this fashion" helps us understand that Jesus was not dictating a new prayer to be recited. Jesus was giving a guideline for prayer; He was showing what the priorities in prayer should be; and He was showing the variety of themes that prayer could cover.*

Let's look at each phrase of this prayer to gain a deeper understanding of how we are to pray.

# Our Father

What do you learn about God as Father in the following verses?
**Deuteronomy 14:1-2**

**Psalm 68:5**

**Psalm 103:13**

What type of relationship is indicated by the use of the word "Father"? Who is related?

## Who is in Heaven

*You may be so used to this phrase that it doesn't have much of an impact. But God makes heaven His home! The earth cannot contain Him. He is great and transcends everything we know. He is One Who is completely different from anything we can imagine. This phrase should remind us of the uniqueness of our God.*

Why is it meaningful and important to recognize that God is in heaven?

## Hallowed be Your Name

This phrase is very closely related to a statement that God Himself made, recorded in Ezekiel 36:23. Please write out this verse.

Please look up the definition for the following word:

**Hallowed: Strong's #37**

**Greek word:**

**Greek definition:**

*This is the first request made in the Lord's prayer. The first word in the English and in the Greek is "hallowed." It's an imperative verb, which is a command. But the Greek has a special type of imperative, used here, which is best translated: "let Your name be hallowed." This type of language shows that the one praying can be involved in the action. God is being called upon to vindicate Himself, as He said He would do in Ezekiel 36:23; but we who pray can participate in making His name known as holy.*

How do you participate in honoring and reverencing the name and nature of God?

## Your kingdom come

*This is an exciting request! It is loaded with anticipation and hope and promises!*
What did John the Baptist announce? (Matthew 3:2)

What did Jesus preach? (Matthew 4:17)

What is the Sermon on the Mount all about? (Look back at Unit 2/Lesson 2 and your copy of the Sermon on the Mount and what you highlighted.)

How is the kingdom of God described in Isaiah 2:2-3?

*There will be a day when Jesus reigns over the whole earth from Mount Zion in Jerusalem, which will be the highest of all mountains. Until that day comes, those who have trusted in Jesus as their Savior can enjoy His reign in their lives.*

If we belong to Jesus, of what can we be assured according to 2 Timothy 4:18?

> The best we can pray for any person or for any cause is that God's kingdom be advanced in that person or that cause. [24]

## Your will be done, on Earth as it is in Heaven

*We could launch a whole new study on God's will. What is God's will? How do we know it for our own lives? You know, while those seem to be hard questions, it's actually more challenging to submit to God's will than to figure out what it is. So, let us pray like Jesus: "Your will be done." Let us cultivate a heart of surrender, submission, and obedience to God's will, and trust Him to lead us accordingly.*

What does Romans 12:2 tell us about how to know what God's will is?

Our Father Who is in Heaven, hallowed be Your Name.

Your kingdom come,

Your will be done, on Earth as it is in Heaven. ᴱˢⱽ

*These three specific requests are totally God-centered. Do you realize that? To pray them in sincerity means denying ourselves and committing ourselves completely to the Lord. This is the prayer of a sold-out disciple of Christ. It's radical!*

Can you pray this prayer in all sincerity? Are there any conflicts of interest between God's desires and your desires?

*The Lord's Prayer, part one: focus on God. The Lord's prayer, part two: ask for your needs. What do you think about that? When we seek God's kingdom first, God will meet our needs. Jesus will return to this concept very soon! Matthew 6:33 is just around the corner!*

## Give us this day our daily bread

What attitude is found in this prayer request and its parallel in Proverbs 30:8?

How will you trust Him to meet your needs one day at a time?

## And forgive us our debts,
## As we also have forgiven our debtors

Please look up the following words:

**Debts: Strong's #3783**            **Debtors: Strong's #3781**
**Greek word:**                      **Greek word:**
**Greek definition:**                **Greek definition:**

*We owe obedience to God and when we come up short, we need to ask for our debts to be cancelled.*

How does Colossians 2:14 say that Jesus handled our debt? (The New American Standard Version says it best.)

---

These verses are a forceful way of making the significant point that it is unthinkable – impossible – that we can enjoy God's forgiveness without in turn extending our forgiveness toward others. [25]

---

*Forgiving those who have sinned against us does not cause God to forgive us. Instead, forgiving others is evidence that we have experienced the forgiveness of God. And once again, as in all of Jesus' teaching in the Sermon on the Mount, our actions are only possible through the power of the indwelling Holy Spirit.*

# And do not lead us into temptation,
# But deliver us from the evil one

*This last request is a powerful and important one. It is stated in the strongest language possible in the Greek. Jesus tells us to pray for protection and deliverance, because we will face extremely difficult situations which may cause a crisis of belief. He certainly knew Peter would go through that type of testing.*

What do we know for certain according to James 1:13?

So how then, are we tempted, according to James 1:14?

And what does Peter tell us in 2 Peter 2:9?

*We must remember that Jesus gave the disciples this prayer as an example, not as a ritual. I know that I have repeated this prayer many times without thinking about what I'm saying. This lesson has helped me realize the significance of these requests.*

Please rewrite the Lord's prayer in your own words as the prayer of a committed disciple.

Lesson Three: Matthew 6:19-24

## JESUS: ON MONEY

*"Put your money where your mouth is." That's not from the Bible, but it's the gist of the next passages. If you confess with your mouth that Jesus is Lord, then the management of your money will reflect your commitment to Him.*

> Depend on the Lord to give you His perspectives
> about your daily needs.

**Please read Matthew 6:19-24.**

The first verses make a comparison between a worldly focus versus a heavenly focus. Please note the differences below.

| Worldly Focus | Heavenly Focus |
|---|---|
|  |  |

The point that Jesus emphasized in Matthew 6:21 was what? It's pretty simple, straightforward language. What does this mean?

*Now we come to some verses that are not so simple and straightforward! On the other hand, they are confusing even to scholars. "The eye is the lamp of the body." Well, that just means that we see with our eyes. But metaphorically, it means that our perspective affects our whole being.*

What kind of eyes are compared in Matthew 6:22-23?

*The Greek word (poneros) which has been translated as "bad" can also be translated as "evil." Near Eastern cultures considered the "evil eye" one that was greedy and enviously coveting what others had. Watch out for the evil eye! If your eyes are green with envy and you are focusing on worldly things, then your desires will affect your whole being.*

What does Matthew 6:23 say will be the effect of the evil eye?

*The Greek word describing the good eye can also be translated as "sincere" or "single," and this leads us to understand that the good eye is one that has a single, sincere focus on things that have a heavenly, eternal value. A single-mindedness is critical in faithfully serving a master as well, which leads us to the next verse.*

What problem will you encounter if you try to serve two masters?

How could money become a master that you serve? What worldly interests could money represent?

*"Where your treasure is, there will your heart be also." "You cannot serve God and money." Something's got to give.*

So, how do you store up treasure in heaven? Look back at the previous verses in Matthew 6. You'll gain heavenly treasure – rewards – from what?

How does 1 Timothy 6:17-19 tell us to store up treasure in heaven?

*The life of a committed disciple will have one single ambition – to love the Lord His God with all his heart, with all his soul, with all his mind, and all his strength. No earthly possession or ambition will take priority over his Master.*

Do you need to have a yard sale to clean out your house and your heart? What's got to go?

*So…if we aren't going to be slaves to worldly things and we are going to be heaven-minded… then how are the bills going to get paid? The disciples probably didn't think in those exact terms, but I expect they wondered how they would afford their tunics and pay Caesar's taxes.*

> The chief reason we are so preoccupied with our possessions and with acquiring more of them is that we worry about the future and do not trust God to care for us. [26]

*We need to hear Jesus' teaching on trusting God – as much today as ever.*

**Read Matthew 6:25-34.**

One command is repeated three times. What is it?

What does Jesus say that we might worry about?

Why shouldn't we worry?

*Have you spent any time bird-watching? As I write this, I'm enjoying a special time of study at the beach. Sea gulls and the other beach birds are hilarious! They run away from the waves just like children, but they also run as quickly as their little legs can carry them as they hunt for food in the sand as the waves wash away. I don't know why they don't fly more. Watching them helps me see the truth of Matthew 6:26 – I can't see what these birds eat – but God sees them and provides for them. And if God provides for them and all of His creation, then, of course, He will provide for us!*

What is the name of the Lord in Genesis 22:13-14? What circumstance revealed it to Abraham?

How did Jesus describe Himself and what does He promise in John 6:35?

*If you are going to trust God with the rest of your eternal life, then shouldn't you trust Him for your life today?*

According to Matthew 6:33, what is to be our top priority – our single-minded focus?

How do verses 33 and 34 relate to each other?

Worry is practical atheism and an affront to God. [27]

*The Sermon on the Mount is all about the kingdom of God and all about living in the right way before God. So – it's a good time for a review.*

If we are seeking the kingdom of God, and His righteousness, then what will be evident in our lives… based on what we've studied so far in Matthew 5 – 6?

*I once heard someone comment on a pastor saying: "That man went from preachin' to meddlin'!"*

What about Jesus? Is He meddlin' in your life? Is He pointing out some areas that you need to change?

# JESUS: ON JUSTICE

*"What goes around comes around." "You're getting a taste of your own medicine." "What's good for the goose is good for the gander." These clichés are all based on Matthew 7:1-5! Let's look at the original teaching.*

> Only the Spirit of God knows the mind of God.
> Depend on Him to teach you today.

**Please read Matthew 7:1-5.**

*Remember that at the beginning of the Sermon (Matthew 5:20), Jesus said that our righteousness must exceed that of the Pharisees. The Pharisees were guilty of being critical, judgmental, and falsely judging themselves, other people, and even Jesus. Followers of Jesus would be different.*

*The command is clear – do not judge. But the reason for the command is clear as well, yet often overlooked.*

Why are we not to judge according to Matthew 7:1?

Please look up the definition for the following word:
**Judge: Strong's #2919**
**Greek word:**
**Greek definition:**

What will happen and when will it happen according to Matthew 7:2?

> The tense of the verb *judged* signifies a once-for-all final judgment. If we first judge ourselves, then we are preparing for that final judgment when we face God. [28]

How did Paul explain this teaching of Jesus in Romans 14:10-13?

*I want God to look at me with grace and forgiveness when I stand before Him. That's the way I need to look at my fellow believers today.*

What examples of righteous, kingdom living have we seen so far in the Sermon on the Mount that we should carry out instead of being harsh, critical, and judgmental?

What are we and who are we like, according to Matthew 7:5, if we don't first examine ourselves?

 It's time to practice! Have you noticed any specks in other believers' eyes lately? Have you stopped to look in the mirror at yourself first? What faults do you have for which you need grace and forgiveness?

**Please read Matthew 6:31 – 7:6.** Give simple answers to the questions below.
What is Matthew 6:31-34 about?

What is Matthew 7:1-5 about?

What is Matthew 7:6 about?

*These three passages don't really seem to be related at first glance. Matthew 7:6 is hard to understand. But Matthew, the precise accountant, was an exceptional writer as well, and the Sermon on the Mount is intricately woven together. Of course, the Holy Spirit really gets the credit for inspiring Matthew. So – if the Sermon on the Mount has been fitting together perfectly so far, then these verses will also be completely appropriate at this point.*

*First, Jesus warns us not to be judgmental (Matthew 7:1-5); and then, He counsels us to be discerning, rather than naïve and gullible (Matthew 7:6).*

*Matthew 7:6 is one verse, written as a proverb, with parallelism. It has four phrases, which correlate to each other as shown below: A and A1, and B and B1.*

(A) Do not give what is holy to the dogs
  (B) Nor cast your pearls before swine
  (B1) Lest they trample them under their feet
(A1) And turn and tear you in pieces.

> **That which is holy** is something commonly recognized as sacred. The reference is to the meat offered in sacrifice. The picture is that of a priest throwing a piece of flesh from the altar of burnt-offering to one of the numerous dogs which infest the streets of Eastern cities.
>
> **Pearls before swine** is a picture of a rich man wantonly throwing handfuls of small pearls to swine. Swine in Palestine were at best but half-tamed, the hog being an unclean animal. Small pearls, called by jewelers *seed-pearls*, would resemble the maize on which the swine feed. They would rush upon them when scattered, and, discovering the cheat, would trample upon them and turn their tusks upon the man who scattered them.[29]

*Vicious dogs and unclean swine were used as metaphors of those who viciously reject the message of the gospel. This proverb teaches us to be discerning and careful not to proclaim the gospel before those who only want to mock or ridicule it.*

How does Titus 3:10-11 teach a similar concept?

Have you ever seen the promises of God ridiculed by those who reject it? How?

*We've had 88 verses of Jesus' sermon on the lifestyle of a citizen of the kingdom of heaven. They have been challenging teachings. However, even though God's standards are high, we should not be discouraged or anxious. We can turn to our heavenly Father for His guidance, His comfort, His protection, and His provision. This is what Jesus reminds us of just before He makes His concluding statements.*

**Please read Matthew 7:7-11.**

| What are we to do? | What will God do? |
| --- | --- |
| 1. | 1. |
| 2. | 2. |
| 3. | 3. |

*While asking, seeking, and knocking may refer to the same types of prayers, it may be that Jesus is indicating a rising intensity in one's prayers.*

*"Ask" indicates coming to God with humility and consciousness of need.... "Seek" links one's prayer with responsible activity in pursuing God's will.... "Knock" includes perseverance in one's asking and seeking. Ask, seek, and knock are imperatives which should be read: ask and keep asking, seek and keep seeking, knock and keep knocking.*

According to Matthew 7:8, who will be answered?

*Don't forget that this is a message to those who are citizens of the kingdom of heaven and know God as their Father. The promise of answered prayer is to those who are rightly related to their Holy God.*

What examples are given to illustrate the truth of Matthew 7:7-8?

1.

2.

3.

*Our Father in heaven knows how to give good gifts. He will answer our prayers with what He knows is good for us. This helps us understand why our prayers are not always answered the way that we expect.*

*Now that we have been assured of receiving whatever we need so that we will be able to follow Jesus' teachings, we can sit back; let it all sink in; and look to God to lead us in righteousness.*

Please take this time to ask, seek, and knock.

*Our next 2 lessons will bring us to the conclusion of the Sermon on the Mount. And then the adventure with Jesus will continue!*

---

Lesson Five: Matthew 7:12-29

# JESUS' GOLDEN RULE

*And now, for the summary of the Sermon on the Mount – in one sentence!*

Pray that you will walk by the Spirit
and not fulfill the desires of the flesh.

Please write out, word for word, Matthew 7:12.

No other teaching is so readily identified with Jesus; no other teaching is so central to the righteousness of the kingdom and the practice of discipleship.[30]

*The first word, "therefore," shows that this verse draws a conclusion from the preceding thoughts.*

How did the Sermon on the Mount begin, in Matthew 5:17? What connection does this verse have to Matthew 7:12?

What does the Law teach? Note what you learn from Leviticus 19:18.

Did Paul agree? See Romans 13:9 and Galatians 5:14 and record his perspective.

What about James? What did he say in James 2:8?

And what did John say about it? See 1 John 4:11, 21.

It's your turn! How would you put the Golden Rule into your own words?

*The bookends of the Sermon on the Mount are Matthew 5:17 and 7:12. Everything in between is summarized by the Golden Rule. Jesus hasn't just given us a list of hard to keep rules, He has been teaching us how to love each other, even as we are loved. And when we are doing good to others, we are imitating our Father in heaven, who does good to us!*

So, let's review the Sermon on the Mount, again! What do you remember from Matthew 5-7 that reflects this teaching – to love others as we love ourselves, doing unto others what we want done to us?

> If this teaching of Jesus were to be lived out in the world, the whole system of evil would be dramatically shaken. Even if it were to be manifested seriously in the Church, its impact would be incalculable. [31]

*Now that the Sermon has been summarized in one sentence, it's time to start wrapping things up. But Jesus doesn't put a pretty bow on His presentation. His concluding remarks are full of warning; our future, eternal lives will be determined by our decisions.*

**Please read Matthew 7:13-29.**

These passages show us three scenarios which contrast true discipleship with lawlessness. Please compare them in the chart below.

| Matthew 7 | True discipleship | Lawlessness |
|---|---|---|
| **Two Gates/ Roads (7:13-14)** | The Narrow Gate | The Wide Gate |
| **Two trees / fruits (7:15-23)** | True prophets (implied) | False prophets |
| **Two builders/ foundations (7:24-27)** | Wise person | Foolish person |

*The wide gate and broad path imply an easiness and comfort for the journey, and the narrow gate clearly leads to a difficult path. The disciple of Christ will encounter a variety of troubles and trials. That's no secret. Jesus declared it at the very beginning of His sermon. But, He guaranteed happiness and the rewards of the kingdom for those willing to endure.*

What does Acts 14:22 tell us?

What do you think about traveling on the narrow path?

*If you will walk with me, and we walk with Jesus, it will be a good journey – even if it's hard. Our destination is worth it. But while we are walking, we may be distracted and endangered by those pretending to belong to Jesus. Watch out for the wolves!*

What do Matthew 7:16 and 20 tell us to look at?

What does 2 Peter 2:1 tell us to watch for?

*During our journey, we must be alert and discerning, and look at the fruit – the works of those who say they belong to Christ. This is the teaching of Matthew 7:15-20. Works must be discerned in the present by disciples, but in the future, words will be examined by Jesus Himself. This is the teaching of Matthew 7:21-23.*

How are those described in Matthew 7:21-23, whom Jesus says He never knew? What did they fail to do? How did Jesus describe their works?

*The phrase at the end of Matthew 7:23 is translated in different ways in the NAS (you who practice lawlessness), NIV (you evildoers), and KJV (ye that work iniquity). None of those translations actually communicate the literal Greek – which with its present participle indicates a regular, ongoing action: "you continually and habitually practice lawlessness" is the idea. This is not the lifestyle of one who has turned her life over to the lordship of Christ and is following His teachings.*

*These warnings are given to us for our own sake. We must examine our lives, so that we can be certain that we are on the right path, and that we are true disciples, and that we truly know the Lord. Don't be deceived by your own religious lifestyle. Are you doing the will of God as Jesus has taught us?*

Perhaps no passage in the NT expresses more concisely and more sharply that the essence of discipleship is found not in words, nor in religiosity, nor even in spectacular deeds in the name of Jesus, but only in the manifestation of true righteousness – i.e. doing the will of the Father as now interpreted through the teaching of Jesus. [32]

# JESUS' AUTHORITY AMAZES

*You know the story. You probably know the song. "The wise man built his house upon the rock and the house upon the rock stood firm!" But now you know the sermon behind the story. Jesus' teaching on the kingdom of heaven and the righteousness of its citizens is concluded with the story that tells us to make wise decisions. Our future depends on it.*

Please turn to the Holy Spirit to lead you to respond appropriately to Jesus' words and authority.

**Please read Matthew 7:24-27.**

What does the wise man do with Jesus words?

What is the wise man like and what happens to him when the storm comes?

What does the foolish man do with Jesus words? How does this relate to Matthew 7:21-23?

What is the foolish man like and what happens to him when the storm comes?

What type of storm is described in Ezekiel 13:13 and what is the reason for it?

*The judgment of God is often described as a storm of some kind. This concluding warning about making wise choices ultimately warns those who do not heed the words of Christ that disaster will come to them. As the previous warnings show, they will experience destruction that lasts for eternity. It grieves me to write this, but it was what Jesus wanted us to know: "the bottom line for those who reject Christ is that they are destined for everlasting torment, destruction that keeps on destroying forever."* [33]

"Thus," remarks Bengel, "it is not necessary for every sermon to end with consolation." [34]

What was the people's reaction to Jesus' teaching according to Matthew 7:28?

Please look up the following word:
**Amazed: Strong's #1605**
**Greek word:**
**Greek definition:**


*This word is a combination of two words that when put together mean to drive one out of his senses by a sudden shock. We might say – I was struck with the incredible beauty of the sunset. Another way to describe the reaction of the people to Jesus teachings would be that they were spellbound, astounded, totally dumbfounded...they were struck out of their senses by some strong feeling, such as fear, wonder, or even joy!*

What caused the people to be amazed?


Please look up the following word:
**Authority: Strong's #1849**
**Greek word:**
**Greek definition:**


*Jesus spoke as the Son of God and stunned His listeners with His assumption that His word was enough. It was. And it still is. Every time Jesus opened His mouth to teach, He spoke with the absolute certainty that what He communicated was truth from God the Father. He had been given the authority to do so. He taught knowing that He spoke the very words of God.*

What did Jesus proclaim in John 7:16?


*Have you been listening to Jesus? Are you amazed? Do you realize that you have heard the very words of God? Consider the power of the word of God:*

Many years ago in a Moscow theater, matinee idol Alexander Rostovzev was converted while playing the role of Jesus in a sacrilegious play entitled *Christ in a Tuxedo*. He was supposed to read two verses from the Sermon on the Mount, remove his gown, and cry out, "Give me my tuxedo and top hat!" But as he read the words, "Blessed are the poor in spirit, for theirs is the kingdom of heaven. Blessed are they that mourn, for they shall be comforted," he began to tremble. Instead of following the script, he kept reading from Matthew 5, ignoring the coughs, calls, and foot-stamping of his fellow actors. Finally, recalling a verse he had learned in his childhood in a Russian Orthodox church, he cried, "Lord, remember me when Thou comest into Thy kingdom!" (Luke 23:42). Before the curtain could be lowered, Rostovzev had trusted Jesus Christ as his personal Savior. [35]

Please read the Sermon on the Mount (beginning on page 28) in its entirety once more. What impact has it had on you?

# Unit Four  Matthew 8:1 — 10:23

Lesson 1  Jesus heals the sick

Lesson 2  Jesus proves his authority

Lesson 3  Jesus gives sight to the blind

Lesson 4  Jesus' compassion and co-workers

Lesson 5  Jesus' commission

Lesson 6  Jesus' strategic assignment

# JESUS HEALS THE SICK

*The crowds were amazed at Jesus' teaching. I hope you were too. But not just amazed... also changed. Jesus taught with the authority of our holy God. And now, He will continue to change lives, as He demonstrates that authority – over nature, over disease, over sin, over tradition, and over men. The miracles of Jesus were proof – that He is the Messiah, the promised One.*

Please pray that the Spirit will increase
your faith to believe in the power of God.

What does Isaiah 42:6-7 say that the Messiah will do?

Please read the next "narrative" section in Matthew 8:1-9:38 and enjoy seeing the authority of the King. As you read, fill in the chart to get the big picture of everything He did. I'll do the first one to get you started.

**Types of miracles include:**

Healing

Healing at a distance

Resurrection

Exorcism

Authority over nature

After you have filled out the chart, answer the following question:

Which one of these miracles would you like to have been an eyewitness to, and why?

| | Reference | Miracle | Type of Miracle | How Faith Demonstrated | How Jesus Performed Miracle |
|---|---|---|---|---|---|
| 1 | Matthew 8:2-4 | Healed leper | Healing | Asked: Lord if you are willing | Touched leper |
| 2 | Matthew 8:5-13 | | | | |
| 3 | Matthew 8:14-15 | | | | |
| 4 | Matthew 8:16 (two types) | | | | |
| 5 | Matthew 8:23-27 | | | | |
| 6 | Matthew 8:28-34 | | | | |
| 7 | Matthew 9:2-7 (2 types) | | | | |
| 8 | Matthew 9:18-26 | | | | |
| 9 | Matthew 9:20-22 | | | | |
| 10 | Matthew 9:27-31 | | | | |
| 11 | Matthew 9:32-33 | | | | |
| 12 | Matthew 9:35 | | | | |

*Matthew described many miracles for us. Being the orderly author that he is, he has given them to us in three sets, with important lessons on discipleship in between each set. Hmmm. Do the miracles correspond to the discipleship lessons? Why, yes! Of course! That's how perfect God's inspired word is.*

Matthew 8:18-22 tells of two "would-be" disciples. When Jesus commanded His disciples to go to the other side of the Sea of Galilee, two followers responded.

The first person was quick to say: _____

What does Jesus' response to him indicate about discipleship?



The second person was hesitant and said: _____

What does Jesus' response to him indicate about discipleship?

> Jesus' pun that the dead can bury their own dead means that those who will bury the would-be disciple's father are dead to the kingdom, not alive to its rigorous demands, which supersede even one's duty to parents. [37]

What kind of disciple are you?



*"Now when He got into a boat, His [real] disciples followed Him." I added a word for emphasis! And Jesus' real disciples will experience the reality that following Jesus includes hardship and following Jesus brings about new priorities. It was time to go sailing. They would need raincoats.*

Lesson Two: Matthew 8:23-9:17

# JESUS PROVES HIS AUTHORITY

*Row, row, row your boat… gently down the stream… merrily, merrily, merrily, merrily… life is but a dream! Well, you're probably just dreaming if that's what you think! There are certainly some great moments, but there are a lot of storms and struggles in our lives.*

*In our last lesson, we saw that true disciples would count the cost of hardship and loyalty to Jesus. The next three miracles show the disciples being tested in these areas.*

> Commit yourself to the Lord,
> entrusting yourself to His sovereignty.

Please fill in the blanks according to Matthew 8:23-27. I want to make sure you notice some key details!

NIV **Matthew 8:23** Then he got into the boat and his disciples _____ him. ²⁴ _____ _____, a _____ _____ came up on the lake, so that the waves swept over the boat. But Jesus was _____ ²⁵The disciples went and woke him, saying, "Lord, save us! We're going ____ _____!" ²⁶He replied, "You of _____ faith, why are you so _____?" Then he got up and _____ the winds and the waves, and it was completely calm. ²⁷The men were _____ and asked, "What kind of _____ is this? Even the winds and the waves obey him!"

Please look up the following word:
**Storm: Strong's #4578**
**Greek word:**
**Greek definition:**

*That was some storm, wasn't it? Big enough and bad enough to scare even four seasoned, salty fishermen turned disciples.*

So who does Jesus rebuke first, and why?

What does James 1:2-3 tell us?

*The storms of life expose our weaknesses, which need strengthening through exercise. Jesus had taught with authority and had healed with authority, but the disciples had not trusted him yet as one with all authority. The quality of our faith is directly related to our understanding of who Jesus is, because He is the object of our faith.*

How's the weather in your life? Is it stormy? How can you demonstrate great faith during hard times?

*Well, they sailed to the other side of the Sea of Galilee and set foot on dry land again. But now Jesus and the disciples meet up with the macabre...two demoniacs living in a cemetery... who were fierce and menacing to anyone who came near. Yikes!*

The demons do almost all the talking in this miraculous account. Read Matthew 8:28-34.

How do they address Jesus?

What are they afraid of?


How do they express that they recognize Jesus' authority?


What is the surprising response of the city?



*With one word, Jesus showed His authority over His opposition. And then, when the city opposed him as well, He left. The disciples apparently just watched it all unfold right before their eyes! But it was a lesson that if their Master could be rejected, then so too could they. And so too can we, if we pledge our allegiance to Jesus the King.*

Are you a loyal disciple? Do you face opposition or rejection because Jesus is your first priority?




*More opposition, coming right up.*

*"So He got into a boat, crossed over, and came to His own city." Matthew 9:1 That would be Capernaum. Home, sweet home...where He probably stayed at Peter's place. And – behold! Wow! The crowds were back, and some friends wanted their friend healed so badly that they lowered him through the roof! We learn that from Mark 2:1-12.*

**Please read Matthew 9:1-8.**

In Matthew 9:2, Jesus sees their faith and makes a shocking declaration. What is it?



*It's a miracle. Hallelujah! Freedom from sin. But, the skeptical scribes were thinking: "this man blasphemes." More opposition.*

Please look up the following word:
**Blaspheme: Strong's # 987**
**Greek word:**
**Greek definition:**

*Matthew expects us to grasp the magnitude of the scribes concern. Only God could forgive sins. Was this Man saying that He was God? Yes, He was.*

Jesus proves His authority to forgive sins and proves His deity by saying and doing what, according to Matthew 9:4-7?

What does Matthew emphasize in verse 8?

*Are you getting the message? Jesus has been given all authority! Over __all__ things.*

Does He have authority over you? How is this evident?

*Matthew himself experienced the authority of Christ in his life, and he shares a brief biographical account of his call. This is one of the discipleship lessons that is found between the miracle accounts.*

**Please read Matthew 9:9-13.**

*Matthew was specifically a "custom house official." This was the worst type of tax collector, and his very title was associated with oppression and injustice. The Jews considered them to be as despised as prostitutes, gamblers, and thieves. They were just "licensed robbers" and "beasts in human shape."* [38]

> According to Rabbinism there was no hope for a man like Levi [now called Matthew]. He was excluded from all religious fellowship. His money was considered tainted and defiled anyone who accepted it. [39]

*To this poor, pitiful, rich man – Jesus said: "Follow me." And Matthew did. Sharing his story at this point in his gospel indicates that he personally experienced the same thing as the paralytic man in the previous verses – forgiveness of sins.*

Based on Matthew 9:9-13, what would Matthew's three-point testimony be?

Before Christ's call:

Christ's call:

After Christ's call:

*Mark 2:14-17 and Luke 5:27-31 show that Matthew gave the great feast in his house. It seems that Matthew's humility showed through in his own account, because he didn't draw attention to his own hospitality.*

Why did Matthew have a big party at his house? See Jesus' comments in Matthew 9:12-13 to get a pretty good idea of the reason.

Matthew did what he could to introduce others to Jesus. What can you do?

*The feasting must have brought about the next question, which was about fasting. We looked at the next verses when we considered fasting as discussed in the Sermon on the Mount. Being a disciple of Christ was totally new and different from being a disciple of John the Baptist or any other rabbi. This is what Jesus explains in the next passage.*

**Please read Matthew 9:14-17.**

Why didn't Jesus' disciples need to fast at that time? Jesus gives three illustrations as His answer. How do these answer the disciples' question?

*I remember when I first read about trying to put new wine into old wineskins. It sure didn't make any sense to me! It's still a challenging concept to grasp and commentators do not agree on their interpretations. All do agree that Jesus is doing something new and is ushering in a new lifestyle of righteousness by faith in Him.*

*My understanding is that the old garment and the old wineskin represent the old traditions, the old ritualistic legalistic ways of the Jewish religion system which had developed over the years. The old ways did not, and could not, refer to the Law of Moses, because Jesus has already told us in His Sermon that He came to fulfill that law.*

*New wine refers to true righteousness, which will be lived out by the power of the Holy Spirit. The new wineskin refers to the new creation of a person who repents of her sin and trusts as Christ as her Savior.* [40]

Are you legalistic about anything, carrying out empty rituals or traditions? Why do you do the things you do?

# JESUS GIVES SIGHT TO THE BLIND

*Are you an orderly, organized person? Do you like sermons with outlines? What about stories... do you read page by page as the author leads you to the climax and then the resolution? Well, you've got a friend in Matthew. He had a purpose and a plan for everything! Here's his outline for Matthew 8 and 9.*

| First 3 miracles | Discipleship lessons | Second 3 miracles | Discipleship lessons | Third 3 miracles | Discipleship lessons |
|---|---|---|---|---|---|
| **Healed leper** | *1. Disciples will encounter hardship* | **Quieted storm** | *1. Jesus forgives our sins and we should share this good news with others* | **Double miracle: raised ruler's daughter and healed woman of hemorrhage** | *1. Jesus' disciples teach, preach, and heal with compassion* |
| **Healed centurion's servant** | | **Delivered 2 demoniacs** | | **Healed two blind men** | |
| **Healed Peter's mother-in-law** | *2. Disciples must put Jesus first above all else* | **Healed and forgave sins of paralytic** | *2. Jesus' disciples live according to His new grace, not old legalism* | **Delivered demon-possessed mute** | *2. Jesus' disciples work hard to bring in the harvest of souls* |

*These miracles proved Jesus' authority and ability to heal leprosy, paralysis, fever, demon possession, chronic illness, blindness, muteness, and even the ability to raise one from the dead. What Matthew has been pointing out is that Jesus has the authority and ability to heal us from our worst disease – sin. He can forgive us and give us spiritual health. The miracle accounts have gone from simple to spectacular! From touching an unclean leper to touching a dead body! Nothing is too difficult for the Lord. And He will touch us with His grace and give us new life if we trust Him as our Savior. I hope you are already healed!*

Ask Jesus to open the eyes of your understanding through the power of the Spirit.

**Please read Matthew 9:18-19.**

What did the ruler do when he approached Jesus?

Why did the ruler come to Jesus?

What did he believe Jesus could do?

I know those are simple questions, but consider what they communicate. What do these observations tell us about the ruler?

*So Jesus follows the ruler. And Matthew leaves us hanging for the outcome, while he tells us about another desperate situation.*

**Please read Matthew 9:20-22.**

What was the woman's problem?

What was her hope?

How was she healed?

What did the ruler and the woman have in common?

*Those who didn't know the stories of Jesus' miracles would have been waiting with anticipation to find out what happened to the ruler's daughter. When Jesus arrived at the ruler's house, he found a noisy crowd of mourners, which often consisted of hired flute players and musicians. This strange detail is included to show us that the family and friends knew that the little girl had died.*

**Please read Matthew 9:23-26.**

How did the crowd respond to Jesus' arrival? Did they think he could do anything?

But what did Jesus do?

*The faith of a father is highlighted against the doubt of the crowd. The desperate, unclean, helpless, hopeless hemorrhaging woman and dead little girl were healed because of faith in Jesus. Two women were healed. Now two men will be.*

**Please read Matthew 9:27-31.**

How do the following verses show that the blind men had faith in Jesus?

Verse 27 –

Verse 28 –

Verse 29 –

---

Blindness was one of the grimmest maladies in the ancient world and was considered to be only a little less serious than being dead…. The Old Testament records no healing of blindness and none of Jesus' followers is ever recorded to have given sight to the blind. [41]

---

*My eyes have just been opened! I must admit that I'm so used to Jesus' healing of the blind that I didn't realize what an incredible miracle it was. But have just a little trouble with your own eyes or contacts, and you'll see how much sight means to you. It meant even more at the time of Christ, as the notes above indicate.*

Do you remember, from our very first lesson, the importance and meaning of the title "Son of David?" What does the use of this title by these men indicate to you about their perspective on Jesus?

*Do you wonder why Jesus "sternly warned them, saying 'See that no one knows it'" ?*

---

Jesus, as God's servant, did not wish for His spectacular works to result in mob mentality that would eclipse His authoritative words and incite the religious leaders and the Romans to view Him as politically subversive. (But one is not surprised when the two men disobey Jesus and spread the story all over that region!) [42]

---

*The third miracle account that Matthew gives us is quite short. It made quite an impact though.*

**Please read Matthew 9:32-34.**

What do you learn from this healing about…

The effect of demon-possession –

The multitudes –


The Pharisees –


*The first two miracles in this group showed great faith on the part of some who knew Jesus. The third miracle, on the other hand, shows the great unbelief and animosity of the Pharisees.*

What does Isaiah 35:4-6 tell you about the time of the Messiah? What do you see in these three miracles that corresponds to this prophecy?


What did Jesus say to the Jews regarding the Word of God in John 5:38-40?


Do you believe what you read about Jesus in the Bible? What about what you read on the Internet or hear about Him on television?


*If you believe that He is Who He says He is, then you will do what He says to do. You will follow Him and others will see that you are His disciple. This is what the final discipleship lesson in Matthew 9:35-10:4 is about.*

Lesson Four: Matthew 9:35-10:8

# JESUS' COMPASSION AND CO-WORKERS

*Are you the kind of person that, when confronted with a challenge, bristles at opposition...or holds your ground...or backs down and walks away? What kind of person was Jesus? All three at the appropriate time, I think.*

*We've just read that the Pharisees said that "He casts out demons by the ruler of the demons." So what does Matthew tell us that Jesus does about this?*

The Word of God has been given to you today.
Pray that you will believe it and obey it.

**Read Matthew 9:35-10:1.**

*"And" is the very first word in verse 35 in the Greek, and it shows us that verses 34 and 35 are related to each other. I'd say Jesus stood His ground and did not back down when He was slandered and opposed by the Pharisees. He did what He came to do.*

What did Jesus come to do, according to Matthew 9:35? Based on word order, what was most important to Him?

*Did this verse sound familiar to you? Jesus continues to do the same thing as was stated in Matthew 4:32: "And Jesus was going about in all Galilee, teaching in their synagogues, and proclaiming the gospel of the kingdom, and healing every kind of disease and every kind of sickness among the people." NAS*

We learn from the Jewish historian Josephus that at this time there were some two hundred cities and villages in the region of Galilee, an area about 40 miles wide and 70 miles long. "The cities are numerous and the multitude of villages everywhere, crowded with men owing to the fertility of the soil, so that the smallest of them contains above fifteen thousand inhabitants." Based on that assessment, Galilee then contained at least three million people, most of whom could have had direct exposure to Jesus. [43]

*Oh, you've just got to love the Greek language. It has nuances that help us get a better picture of things. Jesus was teaching, preaching, and healing. The Greek participle in the present tense indicates that Jesus was continuously teaching, continuously preaching, and continuously healing. He didn't stop. There were a lot of people with a lot of needs.*

The next verse shows us the heart of our God and our Savior. Please fill in the blanks.

**Matthew 9:36** And seeing the multitudes, He felt _____ for them, because they were _____ and _____ like sheep without a shepherd. NAS

How did Jesus demonstrate His compassion in the previous miracle accounts?

What had He emphasized to the Pharisees in Matthew 9:12-13?

The language suggests the imagery of a predator mangling the sheep and throwing them to the ground, and recalls many passages in the Hebrew Bible that speak of Israel as God's flock and Israel's leaders as shepherds. The imagery implies that the religious leaders of Israel are not faithful shepherds of Israel but vicious predators. [44]

Matthew 9:36 tells us that Jesus was moved with compassion, not so much because of the physical needs of the people, but why?

Please read the prophecy given in Ezekiel 34:10-16. Who will rescue the sheep?

*The rescue had begun. Jesus continued His pastoral metaphors by declaring that it was time to bring the harvest in. The crops were ripe and ready to be picked. He wanted more strong field hands to help bring in the sheaves!*

*Jesus' next sermon in Matthew 10:5-42 is His instruction to His disciples to prepare them for their mission trip. The preceding verses were the final set of discipleship lessons that Matthew interspersed between the miracle accounts. Following Jesus would mean teaching, preaching, healing, and showing compassion. Following Jesus would mean working hard to bring in the harvest.*

> It is possible to pray for someone's salvation while keeping them at arm's length. But when we sincerely beseech the Lord to send someone to witness to them, we place ourselves at His disposal to become one of His workers in that ministry. [45]

Please read Matthew 9:35-38 again. There is a critical point which all disciples need to remember. To whom does the harvest belong?

Will you follow Jesus? Will you do what He has asked? To whom do you want the Lord to send His workers?

**Read Matthew 10:1-8.**
What similarities does the disciples' commission have to Jesus' mission? (Make a list!)

Please look up the following words:
**Disciples: Strong's #3101**
**Greek word:**
**Greek definition:**

**Apostles: Strong's #652**
**Greek word:**
**Greek definition:**

What do the order and use of the two words above indicate? (See Matthew 10:1 and 10:2.)

What do Mark 3:13 and John 15:16 tell us about these twelve men?

*There is a letter (not accepted in the biblical canon) that is circulating these days. It evaluates the disciples and their potential. See whether you agree with its perspective!*

---

To: Jesus, Son of Joseph
Woodcrafter's Carpenter Shop
Nazareth 25922

From: Jordan Management Consultants

Dear Sir:

Thank you for submitting the resumes of the twelve men you have picked for managerial positions in your new organization. All of them have now taken our battery of tests; and we have not only run the results through our computer, but also arranged personal interviews for each of them with our psychologist and vocational aptitude consultant.

It is the staff opinion that most of your nominees are lacking in background, education and vocational aptitude for the type of enterprise you are undertaking. They do not have the team concept. We would recommend that you continue your search for persons of experience in managerial ability and proven capability.

Simon Peter is emotionally unstable and given to fits of temper. Andrew has absolutely no qualities of leadership. The two brothers, James and John, the sons of Zebedee, place personal interest above company loyalty. Thomas demonstrates a questioning attitude that would tend to undermine morale. We feel that it is our duty to tell you that Matthew had been blacklisted by the Greater Jerusalem Better Business Bureau; James, the son of Alphaeus, and Thaddaeus definitely have radical leanings, and they both registered a high score on the manic-depressive scale.

One of the candidates, however, shows great potential. He is a man of ability and resourcefulness, meets people well, has a keen business mind, and has contacts in high places. He is highly motivated, ambitious, and responsible. We recommend Judas Iscariot as your controller and right-hand man.

We wish you every success in your new venture.

Sincerely,

Jordan Management Consultants[46]

---

*It was these twelve, uneducated, unskilled, spiritually stunted men that Jesus chose — and challenged — and changed. He gave them authority – exousia – just like He had been given, to carry out God's will and to lead others to the kingdom of heaven.*

Does Jesus' choice of and plan for the disciples encourage you? If so, how?

*Jesus said, "Follow Me." What an invitation!*

---

Lesson Five: Matthew 10:1-42

# JESUS' COMMISSION

*If you were to take flying lessons, you would log many hours under the instruction of your trainer. You would learn the procedures and develop the skills for takeoff, level flight, turns, climbs, descent and safe landing. What to do in the case of an emergency would be a part of your training as well! Eventually the time would come for you to "go solo" and take to the air without your instructor. One more review of the procedures would be a good idea.*

*Let's look at Jesus' instructions to his students who were about to take their first solo mission trip. They would put into practice what they had been learning.*

Pause and pray for the guidance of the
Holy Spirit as you study today.

**Please read all of Matthew 10:1-42.** This is the second sermon which Matthew records for us.

Who are the apostles to witness to according to the following verses?

| | |
|---|---|
| **Matthew 10:5** | Don't go to _____ |
| | Don't go to _____ |
| | Do go to _____ |
| **Matthew 10:17-18** | You will be handed over to _____ |
| | You will be flogged in _____ |
| | You will be brought before _____ |
| | You will be witnesses to _____ |

*Can you read this passage as if you are reading it being spoken to you today? No, not verses 5-15. That would totally contradict the Great Commission of going to all ends of the earth (Matthew 28:19). There is an extremely significant observation and interpretation that we need to make here. Matthew captured what Jesus told His apostles for their first, short-term mission trip, and Matthew also included what Jesus told His apostles for their future world-wide missions. The "behold!" (in the Greek, NAS, NKJV) in verse 16 serves as a break or a transition between the first instructions for the initial mission trip and the instructions for future ongoing missions.*

*Let's look at part one. The words are easy enough to understand, but I still have a few questions about what it all means!*

**Please read Matthew 10:5-15** – the instructions for the short-term trip.

What are your questions?

*Here are the questions that this sermon prompted me to ponder: Who are the lost sheep of Israel? What did the disciples freely receive? What are they to freely give? Who would be a worthy person in a city or village? Why should the disciples stay with that person? Is "shaking the dust off feet" a normal thing or something unusual that Jesus commanded?*

*A little more study and research will help us discover the answers – here we go!*

Who are the lost sheep of Israel?

**Matthew 9:36**

**Matthew 1:21**

**Jeremiah 50:6**

Do these verses indicate a specific group of Jews or the nation of Israel as a whole?

*Jesus' command in Matthew 10:5 showed that He focused His ministry first on the Jews to whom He came as Messiah.*

How did Peter explain this when he preached to the Jews at the Temple in Jerusalem, according to Acts 3:26? (See Acts 3:1, 11, 12 for the setting of Peter's sermon.)

What did Paul say in Romans 1:16?

Do you have a burden for Jews today to know Jesus as their Messiah? If so, how do you demonstrate it?

*We've already noticed in the previous lesson that the message to be preached by the apostles was the same message that Jesus had been communicating: "The kingdom of heaven is at hand." And we've already noticed that the apostles were to do what Jesus had been doing: heal the sick, raise the dead, cleanse the lepers, and cast out demons.*

What had the disciples freely received and what were they to freely give? See Matthew 5:3 and 10:1.

*But if the apostles were not supposed to take money or supplies for their trip and they weren't supposed to charge money for their ministry, then how would they have their needs met? How would they support themselves? Jesus answered those questions.*

What would they eat? What would they drink? What would they wear? Base your answer on Matthew 6:25-34 and Matthew 10:9-12.

> To settle into the house of a "worthy" person (v. 11) implies that the disciples were not to shop around for the most comfortable quarters. In this place "worthy" probably does not refer to a morally upright, honorable, or religious person but to one willing and able to receive an apostle of Jesus and the gospel of the kingdom. [47]

*Remember that the instructions Jesus gave in verses 5-15 were for a short-term, temporary mission trip. They were to travel without the burden of carrying extra baggage, and they were to depend on God's provision through the hospitality of others. His instructions would change when He prepared them for their life-long ministry.*

What did Jesus tell His apostles in Luke 22:35-36? (Notice the context – vs. 14, 34, 39.)

What principles for today can you derive from the instructions given for the apostles' first mission trip?

*The first part of Jesus' instructions ends with something shocking! Unless you are extremely familiar with the culture and prejudices of 30 AD, you won't notice the twist in traditions.*

A pious Jew, on leaving Gentile territory, might remove from his feet and clothes all dust of the pagan land now being left behind, thus dissociating himself from the pollution of those lands and the judgment in store for them. [48]

*Where were the disciples going? Not to the Gentiles or Samaritans, but to the Jews!*

What was to be their response if the Jewish house or city did not receive them or their words, according to Matthew 10:14-15?

*For the disciples to do this to their fellow Israelites would have been scandalous! Alarming! Inconceivable! Jews being treated like Gentiles? This would have been a symbolic way of saying that the apostles were to view those places as pagan, polluted, and prepared for judgment unless they repented.*

Do you think there is a modern day application for this concept? How should you respond when a person or group rejects your message of the gospel?

*This brings us to the end of the instructions for the short-term mission trip. What stands out to me at the heart of it all is a statement that we can carry into each day of our own lives. "Freely you have received, freely give." God's grace is a free gift. The kingdom of heaven is my home. I want to show others how to get there too. It won't be dusty – only delightful!*

Lesson Six: Matthew 10:16-23

## JESUS' STRATEGIC ASSIGNMENT

*What does the future hold for you? What will happen when you follow God's will for your life? Whether the apostles asked Jesus these questions or not, we don't know; but we know that Jesus did prepare them for what was to come. They would experience everything that He would experience. And He tells them to do what He will do.*

**Please read Matthew 10:16-23.**

What are the dangers described in this passage?

*Matthew 10:16-23 describes situations which were not mentioned in the previous section.*

---

There are three differences between verses 5-15 and 16-23 that indicate a future mission.

1. <u>There will be severe persecution (v. 17, 21-23).</u> No evidence exists that the disciples experienced persecution until after Jesus' death, resurrection, and ascension.

2. <u>The disciples will be witnesses before Gentiles (v. 18).</u> In the first discourse, Jesus told them to avoid Gentile territory, to limit their mission "to the lost sheep of Israel" (v.6).

3. <u>There is a reference to the "coming" of the Son of Man (v.23).</u> This seems to refer to a judgment at the end of history.

When we put these points together, they tell us that Jesus anticipated a significant time of witnessing in the midst of persecution.[49]

---

Please look up the definitions for the following words:

**Deliver: Strong's #3860**
**Greek word:**
**Greek definition:**

**Council: Strong's #4892**
**Greek word:**
**Greek definition:**

*You probably know that this is exactly what happened to Jesus. But the apostles didn't know this was the plan. It happened, however, just as He said it would.*

Summarize the account found in Acts 5:12-20, 40-42.

According to the passages in Acts, as well as Matthew 10:16-23, why would the apostles face persecution?

Why did John say that he was exiled, in Revelation 1:9?

*While the first section of this instruction gave specific instructions for the apostles' short-term mission trip, the second section (which continues to the end of the chapter) prepares disciples of every age for what they will encounter.*

How are we supposed to prepare for and respond to persecution, according to verses 16-23? Each verse tells us something.

Please look up the following definitions:
**Shrewd: Strong's #5429**
**Greek word:**
**Greek definition:**

**Beware: Strong's #4337**
**Greek word:**
**Greek definition:**

*Jesus is telling us to bring our "A" game!! Be smart, strategize, and put a good plan into action. We need to get the good news out to everyone. If one person, place, or people-group rejects the gospel, keep moving! There is someone else who needs to hear it. Jesus said, "Endure to the end." Don't quit. Don't give up. Your work is not in vain in the Lord.*

In the passage we've been studying, what challenge, encouragement or perspective stands out to you?

*This section of the sermon ends with a verse that "is among the most difficult in the New Testament canon." [50] "But whenever they persecute you in this city, flee to the next; for truly I say to you, you shall not finish going through the cities of Israel, until the Son of Man comes." Matthew 10:23*

*Scholars have proposed many different explanations of this verse. D. A. Carson summarizes seven of them. I don't think we need to discuss them all!*

*So, in a nutshell "the Son of Man coming" could refer to: 1) Jesus joining the apostles on their short-term mission trip, 2) Jesus coming to the apostles after His resurrection, 3) Jesus' judgment on Jerusalem carried out by the Romans in 70 AD, or 4) Jesus' return to reign as King over the earth.*

What does Daniel 7:13-14 say about the "Son of Man"?

*Matthew uses this phrase 28 times in his book. In each case, Jesus is referring to Himself and this title emphasizes Jesus' identification with mankind – His humanity. God in the flesh. And He says that He will come again, displaying His deity. This is what I think Jesus was referring to in Matthew 10:23.*

What do the following verses tell you about the Son of Man and His second coming?

**Matthew 13:41**

**Matthew 24:30**

**Matthew 25:31**

*He is coming back! It will be a moment of great judgment and a moment of great glory. We will discuss this much more in later lessons. We are still trying to understand what Jesus was conveying to his apostles and what we can learn regarding our mission to share the gospel of the kingdom.*

Please look up the definition for:
**Finish (NKJV – Gone through): Strong's #5056**
**Greek word:**
**Greek definition:**

*"You won't complete the work to be done in the cities of Israel before I come back." That's what I understand Jesus to be saying in this last verse. His invitation to enter the kingdom of heaven must continue to be proclaimed every day and in every place. There is always someone who needs to hear it. And just before Jesus returns to the earth as King, the nation of Israel will still need to hear the good news.*

What did Jesus say in His last breath? See John 19:30. It is the same Greek word as used above.

*When He surrendered His life on the cross, Jesus knew that His mission was finished. He lived His life as the Son of Man in complete dependence upon and in obedience to the Lord God His Father. He became the perfect sacrifice and died in our place.*

He faced death. You face danger. What kind of dangers have you or will you encounter as you share the gospel and live God's way? Are you willing to endure difficulty on account of His Name?

# UNIT FIVE MATTHEW 10:24 — 12:21

# JESUS' LONG-TERM PLANNING

*The next section of Jesus' instructions to His apostles includes long-range forecasting. Following Jesus will be costly. Hard. Sometimes frightening. But there will be a reward for those who press on and preach in Jesus' name.*

Ask the Lord to show you how to apply
the lessons you will learn today.

**Please read Matthew 10:24-42.**

This passage can be divided into the following sections. Please try to summarize the topic covered in each of them. Keep it simple.

Matthew 10:24-25 _____

Matthew 10:26-31 _____

Matthew 10:32-33 _____

Matthew 10:34-39 _____

Matthew 10:40-42 _____

*As we noticed in the previous lesson, Jesus' send-off sermon to the apostles covered a short-term mission and a long-term mission. Because verses 16-42 are regarding the long-term, world-wide mission, the instructions are applicable for us today. So, let's see what this all means for us.*

In Matthew 10:24-25, if we consider ourselves to be the "disciple" and the "slave," then who is the "teacher" and the "master"? Who then is the "head of the house"? And who are the "members of his household"?

Please look up the definition for the following word:
**Beelzebub: Strong's #954**
**Greek word:**
**Greek definition:**

What did the Pharisees say in Matthew 9:32-34?


*We will see an occasion in Matthew 12 where Jesus' power is attributed to Beelzebub.*

What was Jesus warning His disciples of when He said: "if the head of the house has been called Beelzebub, how much more the members of his household?"


*Good grief! I want others to see the power of God at work in my life and through my actions. I certainly don't want others to attribute God's power to Satan. But some people will think that. I've heard some say that Christians are involved in a cult. So what does Jesus say we should do about it?*

For starters, we shouldn't fear those who are falsely accusing us. Why not, according to Matthew 10:26-27? (You may have to think about this and look at a commentary.)


> The truth must emerge; the gospel and its outworkings in the disciples may not now be visible to all, but nothing will remain hidden forever. And if the truth will emerge at the end, how wise to declare it fully and boldly now. Flat rooftops of [Israelite] houses provided excellent places for speakers. In a sense the apostles were to have more of a public ministry than Jesus himself. He told them things in private, some of which they did not even understand till after the Resurrection. But they were to teach them fully and publicly. [51]

*Being falsely accused is a terrible thing. Devoted followers of Jesus have been persecuted and killed over the centuries because of their faith.*

Do you fear death?


According to Jesus, in Matthew 10:28, what is the wrong fear to have and what is the right fear to have? Why?


What does 1 Peter 3:14-17 say that we should do?


**Please go back to Matthew 10:24-30 and read this section again.**

What are we to learn from thinking about sparrows and our hair?

Please fill in the following blanks and look up the corresponding definitions:

**Matthew 10:32-33** "Whoever _____ (#3670) me before men, I will also _____ (#3670) him before my Father in heaven. But whoever _____ (#720) me before men, I will _____ (#720) him before my Father in heaven." ^NIV

_____: **Strong's #3670**
**Greek word:**
**Greek definition:**

_____: **Strong's #720**
**Greek word:**
**Greek definition:**

How important are spoken words in this passage? List every phrase in Matthew 10:7-33 that refers to what disciples say.

*I hope you noticed the comfort and assurance that Jesus gave the disciples regarding their words.*

When we open our mouths to tell others about Jesus, where do the words come from, according to Matthew 10:20?

How did Paul describe this in 1 Corinthians 2:1-5?

What do you learn from the conversation between Moses and the Lord found in Exodus 4:10-12?

How do you feel about speaking to others about Jesus? Are you opening your mouth?

*If you spend time in private talking with Jesus and listening to His words to you recorded in black, white, and red...then you'll be ready to open your mouth. Knowing the Lord, knowing His Word, and knowing what you believe prepare you to be led by the Spirit during those surprising divine appointments.*

Do you need to have a conversation with the Lord, like Moses did? Talk with Him about your concerns and desires regarding talking about Jesus. This includes witnessing to unbelievers, but also other scenarios as well.

*In the next lesson we will discover what happens when we confess Jesus before men and what happens when we don't. The results are eternal either way. Let's make the right choice.*

Lesson Two: Matthew 10:32-42

# JESUS AND DEATH

*Complete allegiance. No shrinking back. Risking your life. It's all or nothing. For eternity. That may seem extreme. Do you think too much is being asked of you? But Jesus did it. For you. And even more.*

*Our previous lesson ended on the topic of confessing Jesus before men. Our private faith is proven to be real when we make it public.*

 Please begin in prayer, with anticipation that the Spirit will teach, convict and comfort you.

But whoever shall deny Me before men, I will also deny him before My Father who is in Heaven. Matthew 10:33 <sup>NAS</sup>

*If you realize that Jesus' life, death, and resurrection provided your only rescue from eternal suffering in hell, then you certainly won't deny him.*

What are the truths of the following verses?
**2 Timothy 2:12**


**Titus 1:16**

*Those who deny Jesus really never knew Him to begin with. Faith without works – is no faith. Intellectual knowledge is not individual dependence.*

Does your whole lifestyle acknowledge that Jesus is your Savior and Lord? Consider your words – do they express your faith, and are they helpful and not harmful? Consider your silence – do you need to speak up? Consider your actions – are you living like the rest of the world lives, or do you have the higher standards that the holiness of God requires?

Words –


Silence –


Actions –


*We will move on to the next passage –which describes the shocking result of Jesus' coming to earth.*

What are the surprises in Matthew 10:34-39? (There's something in each verse!)


*Many Jews in Jesus' day were waiting for the arrival of the Messiah and the wonderful, peaceable kingdom that He would bring about. Today, it is possible to hear a message that Jesus will solve all your problems, but that's not what Jesus said!*

*Matthew 10:34 makes so much more sense when you understand the original language. The old King James Version actually comes the closest to the original: "Think not that I am come to send peace on earth: I came not to send peace, but a sword."*

---

To send (βαλεῖν) Lit., *to throw* or *cast*. By this word the expectancy of the disciples is dramatically pictured, as if he represented them as eagerly looking up for peace as something to be flung down upon the earth from heaven. They expected Jesus to 'throw' peace down – on the earth! But no – he said – he'll throw down a 'sword' …. Not peace, but division. [52]

---

*Jesus used picturesque language to get the disciples' attention! Then He explained what He meant by "the sword." There would be division, conflict, and hostility between the closest relationships.*

Who is to receive loyalty, obedience, and priority – according to Matthew 10:37? How is this loyalty demonstrated?

How do you demonstrate your loyalty to Jesus – your loyalty to Him above your closest family members – in your own life?

Please rewrite Matthew 10:38-39 in first person, starting your sentence with "if."

*This is a life-changing command and statement. It was one of the first verses that I memorized in my discipleship group in high school. I'm eager to consider it more deeply today.*

*"Take" is the Greek word lambano (Strong's #2983). Friberg's Lexicon gives this definition: (1) as bringing under one's control; (a) with the hand take hold of, grasp.*[53] *And Thayer's Greek Definitions says: to take up a thing to be carried; to take upon oneself.*[54]

What is the definition of the following word?
**Cross: Strong's #4716**
**Greek word:**
**Greek definition:**

> "Let the very name of the cross be far away not only from the body of a Roman citizen, but even from his thoughts, his eyes, his ears" (Cicero *Pro Rabirio* 5).... The Roman citizen was exempt from this form of death, it being considered the death of a slave (Cicero *In Verrem* i. 5, 66; Quint. viii.4). The punishment was meted out for such crimes as treason, desertion in the face of the enemy, robbery, piracy, assassination, sedition, etc.... The victim then bore his own cross, or at least the upright beam, to the place of execution. This in itself proves that the structure was less ponderous than is commonly supposed. [55]
>
> Crucifixion was described by the Roman orator Cicero as the most cruel and frightful sentence. It was inflicted for murder, banditry and piracy but most commonly for rebellion.[56]

Death on a cross was punishment for what crimes, based on the commentaries above?

If you are to take up your own cross, then, what crimes against God does this indicate that you have committed?

*I am writing this study on Good Friday. Today in the Philippines, 23 people were nailed to crosses to remember and re-enact Christ's suffering. It was the 24th time for one 49-year old man. The Associated Press reported: "A Filipino penitent is nailed to a cross during yearly religious rituals in San Juan village, San Fernando town, Pampanga province, northern Philippines on Friday April 2, 2010. Filipino devotees re-enacted Jesus Christ's suffering by having themselves nailed to the cross in yearly Good Friday rites frowned upon by church leaders in Asia's largest predominantly Roman Catholic nation." [57]*

*Based on the whole context of Scripture, this is not what Jesus was instructing us to do. Taking up our cross is recognizing and admitting that we were rebels against God and guilty of sin. Taking up our cross is explained further in Matthew 10:39 – "whoever loses his life for my sake will find it."*

Please look up the definition for the following words:

**Loses: Strong's # 622**
**Greek word:**
**Greek definition:**

**Life: Strong's #5590**
**Greek word:**
**Greek definition:**

**Finds: Strong's #2147**
**Greek word:**
**Greek definition:**

How do the following verses describe what, in our lives, must be lost or destroyed?

**Romans 6:6**

**Romans 8:13**

**1 Peter 2:24**

*Taking up your cross and losing your life is dying to self. It's recognizing that the old self, the sin nature, is a rebel against God, and must die.*

*But – eureka!!! That word is from the Greek "heurēka," meaning "I have found;" from "heurisko" meaning to find; from the exclamation attributed to Archimedes on discovering a method for determining the purity of gold in 1603; now used to express triumph on a discovery.*[58]

*The exciting discovery made when you die to self is that you live to God. As you die to self, you are being purified as gold; and you will live in glory with Him for eternity!*

How did Luke state the concept of taking up your cross in Luke 9:23? What did he add that we must remember?

What aspect of your old sin nature has shown a little life lately and needs to be put to death?

*As we come to the end of this lesson, I'd like to share a note on Matthew 10:38-39 from the Word Biblical Commentary. This paragraph sums up these verses in the context of the whole missionary sermon of Matthew 10.*

> Taking up one's cross refers not to the personal problems or difficulties of life that one must bear, as it is sometimes used in common parlance, but to a radical obedience that entails self-denial and, indeed, a dying to self. To take up one's cross is to follow in the footsteps of Jesus, who is the model of such radical obedience and self-denial (cf. 4:1-11).... For the sake of Jesus, and thus the gospel, the disciple is called to follow after Jesus in unqualified obedience to the will of God, even to the point of death itself, which becomes for the disciple the entry into life. [59]

*It all comes down to the self or the Savior. Who are you following?*

Lesson Three: Matthew 11

## JESUS AND DOUBT

*We've been listening in to the special instructions given to the first missionaries and to future missionaries as well. This is the expected calling and lifestyle of every one of Jesus' disciples.*

And it came about that when Jesus had finished giving instructions to His twelve disciples, He departed from there to teach and preach in their cities. Matthew 11:1 [NAS]

*That's Matthew's signal to us – the second section on Jesus' teaching is over. Matthew has demonstrated thus far in his gospel through his record of Jesus' words and His works that Jesus is the Messiah. Now, in Chapters 11 and 12, Matthew presents John the Baptist's uncertainty of His identity and the Israelite's rejection of His authority.*

*Here's the big picture:*

*Matthew 11:2-24 – Israelites are dissatisfied with Jesus (and so their cities are condemned)*

*Matthew 12:1-21 – Pharisees oppose Jesus (and so the Gentiles are offered the gospel)*

*Matthew 12:22-45 – Pharisees accuse Jesus of being empowered by Satan (and the disciples are recognized as His family)*

Please pray that you will be satisfied with Jesus.

**Please read Matthew 11:1-12:50**, following along with the big picture above.

How are the Israelites dissatisfied with Jesus, based on Matthew 11:16-19?

How did the Pharisees oppose Jesus, based on Matthew 12:1-2; 9-10; 14?

What situation occurred and how did the Pharisees respond in Matthew 12:22-24?

*Got the picture? Yes? No? If your answer is no - that's ok, it takes time for these themes to sink in. I just want you to know the value of reading an entire section and looking at context. Now let's see how we can accept, rather than reject, our Messiah.*

*John the Baptist wanted to accept Jesus as the Messiah. He even called Him by that name: Christ (the Anointed One, Messiah).*

What had John expected the Messiah to do, according to Matthew 3:10, 12?

In the gospel account so far, has Jesus done anything like this?

*John had said, "Are you the Expected One, or shall we look for someone else?" John knew God's Word. The Old Testament is full of the expectation of the Messiah: the One who was to come.*

How do the following prophecies describe the expected Messiah?

**Genesis 49:10**

**Numbers 24:17**

**Psalm 2:6-9**

**Psalm 72:8-11**

**Isaiah 26:9**

**Isaiah 35:5-6**

**Isaiah 42:4, 7, 13**


*John expected to see the Messiah show up with the scepter and with judgment.*

In Matthew 11:4-6, what did Jesus tell John to recognize as evidence of His identity as the Messiah and what was Jesus' promise?


*Taking offense, literally, "stumbling" (Greek: scandalizo), refers to a serious loss of faith, spiritual defeat, or apostasy. [60] Jesus encouraged John to believe that He was the Messiah and to accept the fact that it was not time for Jesus to carry out judgment on the wicked. Blessed is he who does not doubt that Jesus is truly the Messiah.*

Do you struggle with doubt about Jesus or God when things don't happen the way you expected that they would? When prayers are unanswered? When your all-powerful God doesn't show His power? When your Savior seems silent?

*"Jesus answered, 'Go and report to John what you hear and see.'"*

*What you hear and see in Scripture is evidence enough. We've been given the record of prophecies about the Messiah in the Old Testament and the record of fulfillment of many of those prophecies in the New Testament. But just like John the Baptist, we must combine faith with what we see. Some say that seeing is believing. But believing is really seeing! "Now may the God of hope fill you with all joy and peace as you believe in him, so that you may abound in hope by the power of the Holy Spirit." Romans 15:13* ^NET

Remember the beginning of the lesson where we observed that the Israelites were dissatisfied with Jesus and the Pharisees opposed and accused Him. What's your status?

Dissatisfied or satisfied? Why?

Opposed to or in favor of? Why?

Accusing (critical/condemning) or accepting (supporting/defending)? How?

*Please read through Matthew 11 again in its entirety. It will be interesting to notice that now, after John's disciples leave, Jesus pronounces judgment on unrepentant cities. (That's something John had been looking for.) In our next lesson, we'll look at the beautiful invitation given at the end of this chapter.*

Lesson Four: Matthew 11:25-27

# JESUS AND DISCOVERY

*We are about to encounter the mind-boggling sovereignty of God. In the verses that we will study, the concept of election and an invitation to salvation are side by side. Mystery and revelation are alongside each other. Matthew has recorded Jesus' prayer, His perspective, and His precious promise. While the sovereignty of God may perplex you, the salvation of the Savior will soothe your soul.*

Let's pay careful attention to Jesus' prayer in Matthew 11:25-26.

To whom did He pray?


*Considering the context of John the Baptist's doubt about Jesus' identity as the Messiah and the Israelites rejection of Him as such, we see that Jesus' recognition of His relationship to God as His Father emphasizes all the more the validity of His miracles and His teachings, which indicate that He* **is** *the Messiah – the Son of God.*

What did Jesus pray? What type of prayer was this?


Please summarize "these things" to which Jesus was referring – "these things" are found in Matthew 11:13-24.


Based on the context of Matthew so far, who are the "wise and intelligent" and who are the "little children"? Who does not recognize Jesus as Messiah and who does?


According to Matthew 11:25-26, who does the hiding and revealing of the identity of Christ and why?


What is your reaction to this?


> The astonishing thing about God's activity is **not** that God acts in both mercy and judgment but **who** the recipients of that mercy and judgment are: those who pride themselves in understanding divine things are judged, those who understand nothing are taught. [61]
>
> Jesus' balance mirrored the balance of Scripture: He could simultaneously denounce the cities that did not repent and [He could] praise the God who does not reveal. [62]

Now let's look at Jesus' perspective. It parallels the essence of His prayer.

The one sentence in Matthew 11:27 consists of 4 phrases. Please write out these phrases as 4 complete sentences.

1.

2.

3.

4.

*God the Father, who hides things from the wise and reveals them to the childlike (Matthew 11:25-26), has given Jesus the Son the authority to reveal the Father to whomever He chooses (Matthew 11:27). Wow.*

One would be hard pressed to speak of the Son in more exalted language than that used in 11:27, which bluntly yet beautifully teaches that the saving knowledge of God the Father comes only through the electing revelation of Jesus, the exclusive mediator of salvation. [63]

Please look up the following words:
**Know: Strong's #1921**
**Greek word:**
**Greek definition:**

**Reveal: Strong's #601**
**Greek word:**
**Greek definition:**

Do you "epiginosko" God the Father? How has He been "apokalupto'ed" to you?

How did John record Jesus' declaration of this truth in the following verses?
**John 14:6**

**1 John 5:20**

The point is that Jesus thus has a unique role as the mediator of the knowledge of God to humankind. [64]

*You can be aware that there is a God. But unless Jesus takes you by the hand, and you follow Him as He leads you to know God personally, you will remain strangers. The truth of Matthew 11:27 has made me all the more thankful for Jesus' revelation of God the Father to me.*

Please read Matthew 11 again now that you have a better understanding of verses 25-27.

Lesson Five: Matthew 11:28-30

## JESUS AND DEVOTION

*We don't have to jump through hoops, climb mountains, make pilgrimages, or keep 613 commandments to get to know God. Jesus tells us something different and makes a promise that He will keep.*

Pray that Jesus' words will refresh you today.

Please read Jesus' invitation, instruction, and promise found in **Matthew 11:28-30.**

Please look up the following word:
**Come: Strong's #1205**
**Greek word:**
**Greek definition:**

*This word was also used in Matthew 4:19 when Jesus said to Peter and Andrew: "Follow (deute) me and I will make you fishers of men."*

What does the word "come" communicate to you?

Consider the following questions based on Matthew 11:28-30:

Who is invited to know God the Father through Jesus? How are they described?

How does Jesus describe Himself?

What does Jesus say that we should do?

What is promised in these verses?

*Oh, what beautiful, wonderful words. They are an invitation to intimacy with Jesus. They are an invitation to know God the Father. They are an invitation to relief and rest.*

*I've just read several commentaries on this precious passage of Scripture. I've learned so much that I've never heard before. I knew that a yoke was an instrument, a tool, used in farming to connect two animals (usually oxen). It was made of wood, hand-hewn to fit the neck and shoulders of the particular animal that was to wear it in order to prevent chafing. The yoke was part of the harness used to pull a cart, plow, or mill beam and was the means by which the animal's master kept it under control and guided it in useful work.* [65]

*The yoke is used throughout the Bible to represent servitude or bondage. The Israelites knew the yoke of slavery in Egypt and the yoke of oppression to other nations.*

*But I didn't know that the term yoke was also used in a positive sense to indicate submission to the law of God. The Jewish Mishnah (teachings on the Old Testament laws) even indicated that Jews were to take upon themselves the yoke of the kingdom of heaven, meaning that they were to submit to the laws of God.*

> The repetition of the Shema (Deut. 6:4-6), as the personal acknowledgment of the Rule of Jehovah, is itself often designated as "taking upon oneself the kingdom of heaven." Similarly, the putting on of phylacteries, and the washing of hands [Deut. 11:13-21], are also described as taking upon oneself the yoke of the Kingdom of God. [66]

Was this a heavy, burdensome yoke according to Psalm 119:14-16, 33-35, 45-48? How was the law of the Lord viewed in these verses and this psalm?

*These Scriptures show us that it was not the law itself that was burdensome. Instead, the overwhelming minutiae of the oral law and traditions, detailed in the 613 regulations of the Scribes and Pharisees, became a heavy, wearisome burden to any who tried to live by them.*

What did Jesus say about the Pharisees in Matthew 23:4-7?

Now look at Matthew 11:28-30 and note the phrases and use of the personal pronouns: I, Me, My.

Look back at the chart on page 49. How does this relate to Matthew 11:28-30?

It is oxymoronic, if not paradoxical, to speak of an easy yoke and a light burden. Jesus did not endorse the oral traditions of the Pharisees, which could obscure the weightier matters of the law (Matt. 23:16-24). But Jesus' yoke is not less rigorous than that of the Pharisees (Matt. 5:20). Jesus is the sole revealer of the Father, and He, not the Pharisees, is the definitive teacher of the Torah (5:17-48). He is gentle and humble whereas they are proud and ostentatious (Matt. 6:1-18; 23:1-12). Their traditions obscure and even transgress the obligations demanded by the Torah (Matt. 15:3,6), but Jesus gets to the heart of the Torah by stressing its weightier matters. The heart of the oxymoron is that His focus on weightier matters leads to a lighter yoke. [67]

What are the weightier matters that Jesus focuses on?

What does 1 John 5:3 say?

*Those who are weary from striving and working so hard to please God and those who have been weighed down by the heavy burden of rules, regulations, and religious requirements will find rest from Jesus. The Greek word for rest, "anapauo," means to refresh or revive, as from labor or a long journey.* [68]

*It is being in the presence of Jesus, being in a personal relationship with Him and receiving His teaching, that gives us rest. It is in learning from Him that we receive rest. What do we learn? We learn to trust Jesus and know God through Him. We learn how to obey the law of God from the heart.*

*The disciples were face to face with Jesus and learned from Him while He walked on the earth. But Jesus had a plan for those of us who wouldn't see Him in the flesh during our lives on the earth.*

**Please read John 14:15-27.** This passage corresponds to Matthew 11:25-30.

If Jesus says that we are to take His yoke and learn from Him, how does John 14:15-27 say that we receive His teaching, and what is the result of this teaching?

*This has been a lesson with lots to think about. Take some time to relax and be refreshed, thinking about what Jesus has taught you today through His Holy Spirit.*

Lesson Six: Matthew 12:1-21

# JESUS AND GOD'S DESIRE

*I just love how God caused the writers of the Scriptures to intricately weave His truths and themes together, while continuing to teach new concepts. If you pay careful attention, you'll see that the narrative accounts in Matthew 12 give examples of the heavy burdens of the Pharisees' traditions, in contrast to the good, easy yoke (the teachings) of Jesus.*

Ask the Spirit to give you
understanding of the Word of the Lord.

**Please read Matthew 12:1-21.**

How many times was the word "Sabbath" repeated? _____

How many times was "unlawful/lawful" or "law" repeated? _____

What can you conclude was the Pharisees' regulation, based on the discussion in Matthew 12:1-8?

*The Pharisees laid the utmost importance on the observance of the Sabbath. Adherence to their minute regulations was their highest concern. "The Mishnah includes Sabbath-desecration among those most heinous crimes for which a man was to be stoned."* [69]

What was God's instruction regarding the Sabbath, and what was His purpose, according to Exodus 35:2 and Deuteronomy 5:13-15? (Other passages regarding the Sabbath are: Exodus 20:9-11, Exodus 23:12, Exodus 31:15 and Leviticus 23:3.)

*Which came first? The chicken or the egg? Which came first? Man or the Sabbath? Which came first? The compassion of the Lord or the law of the Lord? Think about the priorities of the Lord as you consider the next question.*

With what did Jesus confront the Pharisees in Matthew 12:1-8?

*Did you notice Jesus' reference to the temple – the house of God — in His examples of legitimate "law-breaking" regarding the Sabbath? David "broke the law" in the temple. The priests "broke the law" in the temple. Breaking the law on the Sabbath! In the temple of all places! But both David and the priests "broke the law" because they were serving the Lord.*

*And Jesus said, "Something greater than the temple is here." Matthew 12:6 He was speaking of Himself! If the temple was the most sacred place and service in the temple was permissible on the Sabbath, then Jesus was making the statement that He Himself was more sacred and more important than the temple itself. Jesus is greater than the temple. Service to Him is greater than service in the temple. The disciples were innocent of "breaking the law" on the Sabbath because they were in service to the Lord Himself, the Lord of the temple, the Lord of the Sabbath.*

Matthew gives us a second Sabbath encounter. But let's read it first in **Luke 6:6-11.**

Now read Matthew's record of the Sabbath encounter and make notes on what you learn from both passages in the chart on the next page.

|  | Matthew 12:9-14 | Luke 6:6-11 |
|---|---|---|
| Timing |  |  |
| Location |  |  |
| Pharisee's motives |  |  |
| Miracle |  |  |
| Jesus' teaching |  |  |

*Matthew included this second Sabbath incident at this point in his narrative, not because it was chronologically important, but because it was thematically important. It demonstrates the accuracy of Jesus' interpretation of the laws regarding the Sabbath.*

*It's always right to do good on the Sabbath! That's a law which gives freedom! Jesus' yoke is easy and His burden is light!*

Based on God's purposes for the Sabbath given in the Old Testament and based on Jesus' response to the Pharisees in Matthew, how would you summarize the heart of God's desire for proper observance of the Sabbath?

Let's look at Matthew's summary regarding these two incidents. What did Jesus do next, according to Matthew 12:15-16?

*Hmmm. The Pharisees had just set Him up. Tried to trick Him. Challenged Him. Wasn't He mad? Why didn't Jesus confront and condemn them, right then and there? Oh, Matthew tells us why.*

Why did Jesus withdraw and tell others not to tell who He was, according to Matthew 12:17-21? How is the Servant of the Lord described in these verses?

> The servant "will not quarrel or cry out" or raise his voice in the streets (v. 19). The picture is not one of utter silence (else how could he "proclaim" justice [v. 18]? cf. John 7:37) but of gentleness and humility (11:29), of quiet withdrawal (see on vv. 15-17) and a presentation of his messiahship that is neither arrogant nor brash. [70]

*Didn't Jesus just describe Himself as "gentle and humble in heart" (Matthew 11:29)? He is the Messiah as prophesied by Isaiah.*

If we are to take His yoke upon ourselves and learn from Him, what can we learn and apply from Matthew 12:1-21 regarding controversy and confrontation?

*Matthew's quotation of Isaiah 42:1-4 brings a summary to the teachings and events thus far in Matthew 11 and 12. It also provides a critical truth as the background for the next controversy with the Pharisees.*

Who empowers the Messiah, according to Matthew 12:18?

According to Matthew 12:22-32, the Pharisees accuse Jesus of being empowered by whom? Who does Jesus say that the Pharisees are slandering/blaspheming?

*The tension is mounting between the true Servant and the self-righteous scoffers.*

# Unit Six    Matthew 12:22 — 14:21

Lesson 1  Jesus faces pharisees

Lesson 2  Jesus preaches with parables

Lesson 3  Jesus reveals mysteries

Lesson 4  Jesus talks about treasure
and torment

Lesson 5  Jesus explains and refrains

Lesson 6  Jesus feeds five thousand

# JESUS FACES PHARISEES

*Controversy. Accusation. Distraction. Destruction. These are tactics of the enemy. We face these troubles in our lives, and Jesus faced them in His life. There is much to learn from the next passage of Matthew. What did Jesus do?*

Please pray that you will see the deity
of the Messiah as we study today.

**Please read Matthew 12:22-50**. Everything that takes place in these verses seems to have occurred on one particular occasion. Try to see it as a whole event.

What amazing miracle did Jesus do?

How did the crowd respond and what did that indicate?

What was the attitude of the Pharisees, based on Matthew 12:10 and 14, and 24?

Please look up the definitions for the following words (Note: look up in Hebrew!)
**Baal: Strong's #1167**
**Hebrew word:**
**Hebrew definition:**

**Zeboul: Strong's #2073**
**Hebrew word:**
**Hebrew definition:**

*"And knowing their thoughts, Jesus said...." Matthew 12:25. The Pharisees were apparently murmuring among themselves or perhaps even telling the crowds that Jesus was using demonic powers. Matthew doesn't tell us that they spoke directly to Jesus. But He spoke directly to them. Jesus was God in the flesh. Nothing was hidden from Him. He knew their thoughts, their hearts, their motives.*

Jesus spoke to the Pharisees with eternal truth which is also logical! What points did He make in Matthew 12:25-30? What was His important conclusion?

When you face controversy, accusation, or even just a misunderstanding of your perspective, what do you do? (Don't forget what we learned from Matthew 12:18-21.)

*Jesus knew exactly who He was. He was the Son of God. He was the Messiah. And as the Messiah, He had brought the Kingdom of God near to the people of Israel. But they did not accept Him for who He was.*

One of the most serious warnings in all of Scripture is found in Matthew 12:31-32.

What **will** be forgiven?

What will **not** be forgiven?

> **Sin** here represents the full gamut of immoral and ungodly thoughts and actions, whereas **blasphemy** represents conscious denouncing and rejection of God. **Blasphemy** is defiant irreverence, the uniquely terrible sin of intentionally and openly speaking evil against Holy God or defaming or mocking Him (cf. Mark 2:7). The Old Testament penalty for such blasphemy was death by stoning (Lev. 24:16). [71]

*One of the really big questions that we as students of God's Word must wrestle with is: "what is blasphemy against the Holy Spirit?" What is the unforgivable sin? Please recognize the context of this topic. The Pharisees claimed that Jesus' power came from demons rather than from the Spirit of God. Jesus' empowerment by the Holy Spirit and miraculous works should have been conclusive evidence to the Israelites that He was the Messiah.*

> Blasphemy against the Spirit…not only reflected unbelief, but determined unbelief – the refusal, after having seen all the evidence necessary to complete understanding, even to consider believing in Christ. [72]

*Can this blasphemy be committed today? Most commentators that I've read agree: no, not today. Why not? Because Jesus Himself is not walking around in the flesh performing miracles by the power of the Holy Spirit.*

Jesus continued to refute the Pharisees with illustrations and clear truth. How did He warn the Pharisees in Matthew 12:33-37?

*Their words had been clear indications of their evil hearts. Spoken words will indicate what's in our hearts as well.*

What do your words tell others about your heart?

**Please read Matthew 12:38-45.**

*Did the Pharisees still think they could trick Jesus by saying something that sounded religious? They were so badly mistaken. They called Him "Teacher." Now? After accusing Him of casting out demons by demonic power?! And they asked for a sign. Now? After blaspheming the Holy Spirit as a result of the previous sign?!*

How does Jesus describe those who asked for the sign?

What sign was given to them and to what did it refer? (You probably know Jesus' story well enough to recognize to what He was referring.)

*Jesus repeats to the Pharisees that "something greater" is here. He is greater than the temple, greater than Jonah the prophet, and greater than wise King Solomon.*

How had Gentiles responded when Jonah (just a rebellious prophet) and when Solomon (just a wise king) had spoken?

How had the Pharisees responded when one who was greater than Jonah and greater than Solomon had spoken, taught, preached, and performed miracles?

*This whole discussion started (in the evil hearts of the Pharisees) when Jesus healed the blind, mute, demon-possessed man. His illustration in Matthew 12:43-46 now goes back to that same topic. It isn't enough for a person (or a nation, like Israel) to be emptied of something bad. It must be filled with something good or else it will just end up completely worse off than it was before.*

*Jesus was "cleaning house" in Israel as He healed the sick and cast out demons. But unless the people recognized His relationship to God the Father, they would not be a part of His family.*

Matthew concludes this narrative section in verses 46-50 with an unequivocal statement from Jesus. Who are the members of His family?

We do not make ourselves Jesus' close relatives by doing the will of his heavenly Father. Rather, doing the Father's will *identifies us* as his "mother and sisters and brothers." [73]

Are you identified by others as a member of Jesus' family? How?

Lesson Two:  Matthew 13:1-23

## JESUS PREACHES WITH PARABLES

*Let's go to the beach today. Jesus is going to be there!*

Please take time to pray before your study today.
Studying the parables is both simple and hard.

Please read the following verses from Matthew 13 and note the <u>setting</u>, the <u>different audiences</u>, and the <u>general content</u> for the "sermon by the sea."

**Matthew 13:1-3**

**Matthew 13:10**

**Matthew 13:34**

**Matthew 13:36**

*"On that same day…" Please notice that the sermon in Matthew 13 took place on the same day as the events of Matthew 11 and 12. The most important rule regarding interpretation of parables is that they must be considered in context of the situation. Matthew 11 and 12 showed us that the rulers as well as the people of Israel, even Jesus' own family, rejected Him.*

*This was a turning point in His ministry. Jesus continued teaching so that those who did believe in Him could know and understand more. The parables were the way that Jesus could explain more; all the people could hear His teaching, but only those who truly were seeking truth and trying to understand Jesus would learn from Him. Those who had understanding would gain more understanding. Those who rejected Him would continue to do so and would not understand the parables.*

**Please read all of Matthew 13.** I want you to become aware of all the parables and notice that they are all about the kingdom of heaven.

Fill in the blanks below according to the verses given from Matthew 13. Keep it simple. You don't have to give explanations!

The word of the kingdom is like a: _____(vs.18-23)


The kingdom of heaven is like: _____(vs.24-30)


The kingdom of heaven is like: _____(vs.31-32)


The kingdom of heaven is like: _____(v.33)


The kingdom of heaven is like: _____(v.44)


The kingdom of heaven is like: _____(v.45)


The kingdom of heaven is like: _____(vs.47-50)


The scribe who is instructed concerning the kingdom of heaven is like:

_____(v.52)


The disciples wondered why Jesus was speaking in parables to the crowds. His explanation is appropriate for us as well. How would you summarize Matthew 13:11-16?

*Jesus had just said to the Pharisees: "if I cast out demons by the Spirit of God, then surely the kingdom of God has come upon you" (Matthew 12:28). These parables explain the mystery of the kingdom of heaven. Those who have accepted Jesus as the Son of God will understand them and those who haven't, won't. The mystery is that the kingdom of heaven includes a period of time where Jesus' followers (also known as the church) experience the reign of Christ.*

*The Jews were looking for a physical kingdom with the Messiah reigning on the throne over all the earth. That time is coming! But because the Jews rejected Jesus, that wonderful, peaceful kingdom has been delayed until Jesus comes again. The Jews will accept Him as Savior and Messiah the next time He comes (Zechariah 12:10-14).*

*So until then, we need to understand what the kingdom of heaven is like right now.*

In the Parable of the Sower, Matthew 13:3-8, 18-23, how does Jesus explain what the following aspects of the parable mean?

Seed -

Birds -

Devoured -

Stony places -

Scorched and withered -

Thorns -

Choked -

Good soil -

Bears fruit –

The most important point of any parable is its conclusion. If that's the case in the Parable of the Sower, what is its main point?

Now let's make that personal. If you understand this parable and you are a citizen of the kingdom of heaven, what will your life look like? (And what will it <u>not</u> look like?)

*You know what? Jesus has made that same point a few times already! According to the Sermon on the Mount, your life will be salt and light, you'll keep the heart of the law (Matthew 5-7). As a disciple, you'll leave everything to follow Him (Matthew 8-9). As a missionary, you'll trust the Lord for every need and endure persecution (Matthew 10.) On the Sabbath, you'll do good (Matthew 11). And as a member of His family, you will do the will of God (Matthew 12).*

*The Parable of the Sower serves as an introduction to the rest of the parables. It parallels the explanation that Jesus gave regarding why He taught in parables (Matthew 13:11-15). How do we know that? You'll see as you answer the next questions.*

What connecting word is used in Matthew 13:18? _____

What words are used in Matthew 13:19 which were used in Matthew 13:13-15?


*I wish you could read it in Greek! The sentence begins with an emphatic "you therefore" and is followed by an imperative "listen!"*

*The four soils represent four types of reception to the message of the kingdom. The religious leaders and Jewish people had rejected Jesus and His gospel message and were depicted by the 3 unfertile soils. The true disciples accepted Jesus, received His message, and therefore were able to understand more truth about the kingdom. Further understanding would lead to abundant fruit-bearing.*

**Please reread Matthew 13:13-15** and write out a prayer asking the Lord to make your eyes, ears, heart, and mind ready to receive and understand His teaching.




*We are now prepared to hear and understand the rest of the parables!*

Lesson Three: Matthew 13:24-43

## JESUS REVEALS MYSTERIES

*There are more seeds and more sowing in today's parable. But they don't have the same meaning as they did previously.... I'm so glad that Jesus clearly explained this one. I think you'll find it shocking and sobering.*

> Pray that the Spirit will give you understanding as
> we study the mysteries of the kingdom of God.

*Before we go any further, I'd like to give you another tip regarding the interpretation of parables as we continue in this chapter. While a parable is told from real life, it isn't a handbook on how to perform real-life functions; instead, real life becomes an example of spiritual truth. A parable is a teaching based on how things are already done, not a teaching on how they should be done. The parable of the sower (Matthew 13:3-9) doesn't teach a farmer how to plant seed. It tells a story based on what already happens in real life. Then a parable adds an improbable, exaggerated, or even shocking conclusion to lead its listeners to respond to what they've heard.*

So what's the story being told, according to Matthew 13:24-30?

Who?

What?

When?

---

**Tares: (Greek:** *zizánia*): *Zizania* is equivalent to Arabic *zuwān*, the name given to several varieties of darnel - *Lolium temulentum*. The "bearded darnel" is the one most resembling wheat, and has been supposed to be degenerated wheat. On the near approach of harvest, it is carefully weeded out from among the wheat by the women and children. [74]

---

*I'm not a farmer, and I'm not even a good gardener. But I really don't like weeds. And to think that someone would intentionally scatter seeds of weeds in his enemy's field!! Ugh. That was actually done in the Middle East out of spite or revenge when someone wanted to destroy or reduce the value of another's crop. It was a common enough crime for the Romans to have had a specific law against it. Servants would make every effort to get rid of the weeds when they appeared. But in this story – wait! The landowner said they should leave them to grow in the field until harvest time. That part of the story would have come as quite a strange ending.*

*The disciples heard this parable with the crowds and had to wait until they went into the house with Jesus to hear its explanation (Matthew 13:36). You'll have to be patient too. Matthew wants us to hear two more parables first.*

**Read Matthew 13:31-32.**

Consider the following questions to understand how the kingdom of heaven is like a mustard seed. Remember – real life is being given as an example of spiritual truth. And remember, Jesus is revealing a mystery, something new, about the kingdom.

How is the mustard seed described and how would this describe the kingdom?

What happens to the seed and therefore what will happen to the kingdom?

What is the end result (and the main point of the parable)?

Read Matthew 13:33. What was the woman's recipe for bread?

> **Three pecks (NAS), or three measures (NKJ):** This measure was a "saton," the Greek name for the Hebrew term "seah." Three of these was a very large quantity of flour, since a saton is a little over 16 pounds of dry measure. So this was over 48 pounds of flour total, enough to feed over a hundred people. [75]

What does this parable tell you about the kingdom of heaven? How does it relate to the previous parable?

*What's new and surprising about the kingdom of heaven based on these two brief parables? The kingdom is not being ushered in with great pomp and circumstance, as the Jews expected it to be. Instead, the kingdom has begun by something – someone – seemingly insignificant and yet it will have phenomenal growth and prosperity in the end.*

Why is it important for us to know that the kingdom of heaven will have extraordinary growth?

How are you participating in the growth of the kingdom?

*I'm very glad that Matthew gave us these two parables to consider before moving on to the interpretation of the parable of the tares. Jesus confirms that the kingdom of heaven is going to have great growth even though an enemy is trying to do it damage!*

What does Matthew remind us of in Matthew 13:34-36?

*"...and he did not say anything to them without using a parable."* The imperfect verb tense is used here in the Greek, which would be better translated as: *"and He continued to say nothing to them apart from using a parable."* From this point on in Jesus' ministry of preaching and teaching on the kingdom of heaven, when He speaks to the crowds, it will only be in parables. You can see this for yourself by looking at the following verses: *Matthew 15:10-11, 15-20; 16:1-4; 21:23-45, 22:1-2. (That's an optional exercise!)*

---

Jesus told parables to both reveal truth and to hide it. [76]

◈ The parables reveal truth by clarifying difficult concepts ("mysteries," e.g.). Jesus wanted to make known the truth about God's kingdom and values. The revelation was given to disciples — those who positively responded to Jesus and His message and therefore had ears to hear. A positive response to Jesus would get more teaching and more explanation of His parables (Matthew 13:10-23; 36-43).

◈ The parables conceal truth from those whose hearts are hardened against God. So parables were either left unexplained to them or the parables' truths, while understood on the surface, were rejected and served to further harden their hearts, securing their lost estate.

---

*Now, back to those weeds in the wheat.*

According to Jesus (Matthew 13:37-43), what are the analogies in this parable? You'll probably want to reread Matthew 13:24-30 first.

The sower –

The seed –

The field –

The weeds –

The enemy –

The harvest –

The harvesters –

The gathering and burning of the weeds –

The gathered wheat in the barn –


How did the farmer recognize that there were weeds in his field? Based your answer on the parable and its explanation.


Why was a person condemned and cast into the fiery furnace according to Daniel 3:6, 11, and 15?

To whom is given authority, glory, and a kingdom in Daniel 7:13-14? (Note the specific title used here.) What is to be the response of all people to this?

At the end of the age, what will those who are resurrected to eternal life be like, according to Daniel 12:2-3?

*Jesus knew His Old Testament stories and prophecies, didn't He? His parable revealed the mystery that the prophets didn't know: the kingdom of heaven would have a period of time where the wicked coexist with the righteous. The prophets had expected the Son of Man, the Messiah, to judge the wicked at His arrival. That He will do – when He arrives as the Conquering King of Kings. But He came first as the Son of Man, one made in the likeness of a man, one who came to serve and suffer and save.*

So, based on this parable of the wheat and the weeds, should we be pulling weeds right now? Why or why not?

*"He who has ears to hear, let him hear." This is the third time that Jesus has given this exhortation (Matthew 11:15, 13:9, 13:43). It's an allusion to an Old Testament instruction (Ezekiel 3:27).*

You who have ears – what have you heard, learned, or understood in the four parables we've looked at so far? What perspectives do they give you regarding the kingdom of heaven?

---

Lesson Four: Matthew 13:44-58

## JESUS TALKS ABOUT TREASURE AND TORMENT

*Are you beginning to gain an understanding of Jesus' teaching on the kingdom of heaven? It's only been a vague concept to me in the past, but it's becoming clearer now. I'm also finding that the parables make much more sense to me from studying them in context with the previous chapters of Matthew, and I understand them better by looking at them in relationship to each other. It's not a very good idea to just take one parable and study it all by itself!*

*We have four more parables today. I'm praying to have ears to hear.*

**Please read Matthew 13:44-46.**

*The kingdom of heaven is like...something beautiful and precious. These two parables, given side by side, emphasize the same thing.*

What did the man who found the treasure in the field do?

What did the merchant who was seeking beautiful pearls do?

*Imagine – selling everything you have – for **one** pearl. That actually sounds ridiculous. How could **one** pearl be worth **everything**? This is the surprise of this parable and of the hidden treasure parable as well.*

If you are the buyer of the field, or the merchant seeking pearls, and the kingdom of heaven is the treasure, or the pearl, then how would you explain the meaning of these two parables?

*These two parables are only found in Matthew. I've wondered why. Perhaps Matthew the tax collector, who had previously focused on worldly wealth, understood better than anyone that the kingdom of heaven was worth giving up every penny.*

*The greatest treasure is truly worth the greatest sacrifice. And in losing all, you will gain even more than you had. This is the paradox that is biblically and eternally true.*

What did Jesus already tell the disciples in Matthew 10:38-39?

*We will soon see that Jesus practices what He preaches. You are His treasure, and He was willing to give up everything for you.*

*There are two more parables in this chapter on the mysteries of the kingdom of heaven. What's the next surprise?*

**Please read Matthew 13:47-50.**

> The net (Greek: sagene) is not the small one used by anglers to land a hooked fish but a large net or seine with weights on the bottom and floats on the top that encircles many fish. Such a net could contain hundreds of fish and require a great deal of effort to haul in. [77]

Based on verses 47 and 48, what would you understand to be the regular practice of fishermen?


And according to Jesus' explanation in verses 49 and 50:

The sorters are the:

The sorting of fish is:

The bad fish are the:

The good fish are the:

Throwing the bad fish away indicates:


*So what's the mystery in this parable? I didn't recognize it until I learned that the Jews were expecting the Messiah to separate the good from the bad **before** the coming of the kingdom.*

Now that you have that piece of information, how would you explain the mystery that Jesus revealed in His explanation of the parable?


*Do you realize that Jesus has been describing the mysteries of the age that we now live in? The Messiah has already come, and His reign has begun. And in His kingdom right now, there are wheat and tares, good fish and bad - true disciples and false. Jesus has been challenging every listener to make sure he (or she) is for real! He's been doing it since His first sermon.*

Review the following Scriptures and previous lessons to see Jesus' continuous exhortations.

What did we learn from His comments about salt? (Matthew 5:13)


What did we learn from His comments about trees? (Matthew 7:17-20)


What did we learn from His comments about the words and wonders of some people? (Matthew 7:21-23)

So, do you think that everybody that goes to church is going to heaven? Is wearing a cross necklace the same as carrying your own? Can someone think that they are a Christian and not actually be one?

*The warnings given by Jesus are the clearest and severest possible. Those who are not truly His disciples will truly suffer for eternity.*

> Perhaps no doctrine is harder to accept emotionally than the doctrine of hell. Yet it is too clear and too often mentioned in Scripture either to deny or to ignore. Jesus spoke more of hell than any of the prophets or apostles did – perhaps for the reason that its horrible truth would be all but impossible to accept had not the Son of God Himself absolutely affirmed it. It had special emphasis in Jesus' teaching from the beginning to the end of His earthly ministry. He said more about hell than about love. More than all other teachers in the Bible combined, He warned men of hell, promising no escape for those who refused His gracious, loving offer of salvation. [78]

Highlight the references to hell and eternal suffering in the following verses. (All from NKJV.)

**Matthew 5:22** But I say to you that whoever is angry with his brother without a cause shall be in danger of the judgment. And whoever says to his brother, "Raca!" shall be in danger of the council. But whoever says, "You fool!" shall be in danger of hell fire.

**Matthew 5:29** If your right eye causes you to sin, pluck it out and cast *it* from you; for it is more profitable for you that one of your members perish, than for your whole body to be cast into hell.

**Matthew 5:30** And if your right hand causes you to sin, cut it off and cast *it* from you; for it is more profitable for you that one of your members perish, than for your whole body to be cast into hell.

**Matthew 7:13** Enter by the narrow gate; for wide *is* the gate and broad *is* the way that leads to destruction, and there are many who go in by it.

**Matthew 8:11-12** And I say to you that many will come from east and west, and sit down with Abraham, Isaac, and Jacob in the kingdom of heaven. [12]But the sons of the kingdom will be cast out into outer darkness. There will be weeping and gnashing of teeth.

**Matthew 10:28** And do not fear those who kill the body but cannot kill the soul. But rather fear Him who is able to destroy both soul and body in hell.

**Matthew 11:23-24** And you, Capernaum, who are exalted to heaven, will be brought down to Hades; for if the mighty works which were done in you had been done in Sodom, it would have remained until this day. [24]But I say to you that it shall be more tolerable for the land of Sodom in the day of judgment than for you."

**Matthew 13:41-42**   The Son of Man will send out His angels, and they will gather out of His kingdom all things that offend, and those who practice lawlessness, ⁴²and will cast them into the furnace of fire. There will be wailing and gnashing of teeth.

**Matthew 13:49-50**   So it will be at the end of the age. The angels will come forth, separate the wicked from among the just, ⁵⁰and cast them into the furnace of fire. There will be wailing and gnashing of teeth.

**Matthew 16:18**   And I also say to you that you are Peter, and on this rock I will build My church, and the gates of Hades shall not prevail against it.

**Matthew 18:9** And if your eye causes you to sin, pluck it out and cast *it* from you. It is better for you to enter into life with one eye, rather than having two eyes, to be cast into hell fire.

**Matthew 22:12-13**   ¹So he said to him, "Friend, how did you come in here without a wedding garment?" And he was speechless. ¹³Then the king said to the servants, "Bind him hand and foot, take him away, and cast *him* into outer darkness; there will be weeping and gnashing of teeth."

**Matthew 23:15** Woe to you, scribes and Pharisees, hypocrites! For you travel land and sea to win one proselyte, and when he is won, you make him twice as much a son of hell as yourselves.

**Matthew 23:33** Serpents, brood of vipers! How can you escape the condemnation of hell?

**Matthew 25:30**   And cast the unprofitable servant into the outer darkness. There will be weeping and gnashing of teeth.

**Matthew 25:41**   Then He will also say to those on the left hand, "Depart from Me, you cursed, into the everlasting fire prepared for the devil and his angels."

**Matthew 25:45-46**   Then He will answer them, saying, "Assuredly, I say to you, inasmuch as you did not do *it* to one of the least of these, you did not do *it* to Me." ⁴⁶And these will go away into everlasting punishment, but the righteous into eternal life.

What details do you observe about hell from the verses above?

*I deserve the eternal torment of hell. In the five hours that I've been awake today, I've been self-centered and negligent to thank God for His overwhelming goodness to me. But the greatest Hero has made the greatest rescue from the greatest torment. And He provided a way for me to gain the greatest treasure; that treasure that is worth giving up everything.*

Are you a true disciple of Christ? Have you been rescued from the danger of hell? Is there anything that you need to surrender, sacrifice, or abandon in order to gain the greatest treasure of eternal life in the kingdom of heaven?

---

 Lesson Five: Matthew 13:51-58

# JESUS EXPLAINS AND REFRAINS

*We've been listening to Jesus' parables...those simple real life stories with a twist. They're interesting and intriguing. I hope that reading them and studying them in context of what Matthew has written so far has helped you grasp their meaning. Jesus wants His disciples to understand!*

The Word of God has been given to you.
Pray that you will receive it and respond to it.

What did Jesus say to the disciples and how did they respond in Matthew 13:51?

*Ah, what confidence! Well, if they (and we) understand the mysteries of the kingdom, then they (and we) have a responsibility – made clear in one final parable. "Therefore...."*

What is a disciple of the kingdom like, according to Matthew 13:52, and what does he do?

Please look up the definition for the following word:
**Scribe: Strong's #1122**
**Greek word:**
**Greek definition:**

> ...among the Jews the term had long carried the distinctive connotation of a man who was a learner, interpreter, and teacher of the law, God's revealed Word that we now call the Old Testament. Although the scribes and rabbis had added so much tradition that it subordinated and often contradicted God's true Word, their purported task was to study and interpret Scripture. [79]

Based on this understanding of scribes, what would be the scribes' treasure?

If the "old things" refers to the first delivery of God's Word, the Old Testament, then what would the "new things" refer to? (The New Testament is not the answer!)

*It is surprising that Jesus called His twelve uneducated, unskilled, spiritually stunted men – scribes! Another mystery of the kingdom revealed! Jesus can take anyone from anywhere and make anything He wants out of them. The disciples would become the teachers of the truths of the gospel which were based on and intricately tied to the truths of the Old Testament. The disciples, who understood "all these things" about the kingdom of heaven, would be theologians. The "new things" that they treasured were Jesus' teachings!*

Some of the disciples actually became writers of their treasures. Can you name them?

As a disciple with the completed revelation of God's Word available to you, what are you to do with what you have?

*Jesus is about to move on from this location, and Matthew is about to move on to describe some remarkable events. I hope you have been able to see that Matthew 11, 12, and 13 showed us a turning point in Jesus' ministry.*

*The parables of the mysteries of the kingdom (Matthew 13) followed the controversy with the Pharisees and their rejection of the clear evidence that Jesus is the Messiah – the Son of God. Jesus said: "If I cast out demons by God, then the kingdom of God has come upon you." The Pharisees were given demonstrations that the King of the Kingdom (who is mighty in power) was present. His rule had begun, but they didn't believe it — or want it. They rejected Him.*

*And they were not the only ones.*

**Please read Matthew 13:53-58.**

Where did Jesus go?

What did Jesus do?


What was the response?


> The Greek *eskandalizonto en auto* which has been translated as "they took offense at Him" could be translated "they were stumbling because of Him," or "they fell into sin because of him." The verb *skandalizo* occurs rather frequently in Matthew to describe serious sin, unbelief, and apostasy (cf. Matt. 5:29,30; 11:6; 15:12; 17:27; 18:6,8,9; 24:10; 26:31,33). [80]

*The very sad point of this hometown visit is that once again, Jesus is rejected. This time – by those who "knew Him way back when." The homefolks of Nazareth saw that Jesus did miracles and taught with authority, but they remained skeptical. From that precarious point of skepticism, they stumbled and fell into unbelief which is serious sin.*

What was Jesus response to the situation according to Matthew 13:58?



*Please note carefully that Matthew said: He "did not," rather than He "could not." There was no change in Jesus' ability. He reacted as He had toward the Pharisees. Signs and miracles had already been demonstrated and rejected. So now, in Nazareth – Jesus does not perform miracles to counteract unbelief.*

This is a good time to check our reactions to Jesus. He has shown Himself to be the King. Are you submitting to His rule in your life? Consider the following hindrances and check any that apply:

**Like the Pharisees:**

o   You want to be in control

o   You like having power and prestige

o   Tradition is important to you


**Like the homefolks of Nazareth:**

o   You are skeptical that a man could be God

o   You like things the way they are

o   You don't like what Jesus tells you to do

o   You don't want your sins exposed

*It's so easy to distance ourselves from the "bad guys" in the Bible. You know – the Pharisees and Sadducees and Herod and those who rejected Jesus. But we can be just like them sometimes. This study of Matthew continually challenges me to examine my relationship with Jesus. Am I really following Him? Am I surrendering all? All the time?*

Jesus is the teacher. He is the carpenter's son. He is a prophet. And He is the King! It's time for you to have a little talk with Jesus. It helps me express my thoughts (and see both the good and the bad) when I write them down. What do your actions say about your attitude about Jesus?

---

Lesson Six:  Matthew 14:1-21

# JESUS FEEDS FIVE THOUSAND

*We've seen the rejection of Jesus. We've seen His first reactions. Now we will see even more. It's all a part of God's plan. The tide has turned. There's been a tectonic shift — a watershed moment. Jesus knows it and is going to prepare the disciples for what is to come. The cross is set before Him and He will walk resolutely towards it until He lays His life down on it.*

*Before we see more of Jesus' reactions to His rejection, we'll get a glimpse from Matthew of what has happened to John the Baptist.*

Please pray that the Holy Spirit will
show you the identity of the Messiah today.

**Please read Matthew 14:3-12.**

What is the point of this brief account? Who did what to whom?

Now look back at Matthew 14:1-2. John the Baptizer was dead, and what did Herod say about Jesus?

*Matthew has just given us another example of the rejection of Jesus. King Herod doesn't believe He is the Messiah either. He'd rather attribute His mighty works to John the Baptist. That way, Herod's reign as king stays intact, from his perspective.*

*Let's see what the true King does now. What a difference there is between Herod's birthday banquet and Jesus' banquet at Bethsaida.*

Please read the rest of Matthew 14:13-36. Don't rush. You are probably familiar with these events. Worship the King as you see His goodness and greatness.

What do you learn about Jesus from Matthew 14:13-14?

Was there any response to Jesus' compassion from the multitudes?

What do you learn about Jesus from Matthew 14:15-21?

Was there any response to Jesus from the multitudes?

*This is the only miracle performed by Jesus that is recorded in all four gospels. Fascinating. What was it about this particular event that caused Matthew, Mark, Luke and John to think something like: "I've got to tell them about when Jesus created enough bread and fish to satisfy more than 5000 men!"? You can read Mark 6:30-44 and Luke 9:10-17 if you'd like. We'll look at John's account soon.*

*Was there something about the miracle of feeding 5000 men (and more mouths than that when you consider that women and children were eating too) that was more than an amazing act of provision? Matthew has already given us a clue.*

What did Jesus declare in Matthew 8:11?

---

The phrase, "shall sit down," in the original, refers to the manner of sitting at meals; and the enjoyments of heaven are described under the similitude of a feast or banquet - a very common manner of speaking of it (Matt. 26:29; Luke 14:15; Luke 22:30). It is used here to denote felicity, enjoyment, or honor. [81]

---

*I love the New King James Version (NKJV) of the Bible; but if you read the previous verse in that translation or the New American Standard (NAS), you would miss the actual meaning of "sit down."*

Please read Psalm 107:1-9. This psalm rehearses the history of Israel and God's goodness to them and it gives hope for what He will do through the Messiah. What similarities do you see to Jesus' feeding of the 5000?

Now let's read John's account. He includes Jesus' commentary on the miracle which was given to the people the next day. Read John 6:1-51.

How did the people respond to Jesus according to the following verses?

**John 6:14-15**

**John 6:26**

**John 6:30**

**John 6:36**

**John 6:41-42**

> The feeding of the five thousand is an indication to the Jews that the Messiah is in their midst, offering to them – as in the miracle of manna in the wilderness – the reality of salvation, the fulfillment of the promises. [82]

What did Jesus emphasize that the people must do according to John 6:29 and 47?

*Wow! Everything that Jesus does is an indication of Who He Is! That's not that surprising to us now. But back then, the people did not recognize Him. Even when they saw the miracles and considered Jesus as someone from God, they still refused to accept Him as the Son of God and promised Messiah.*

*But He is the One! And He is more than capable of meeting our every need. He is the only one in the world, in this life, in eternity – who can satisfy the hunger of your soul. Chris Tomlin says it well in his song "Enough."*

All of You is more than enough for all of me
For every thirst and every need
You satisfy me with Your love
And all I have in You is more than enough

You're my sacrifice
Of greatest price
And still more awesome than I know
You're the coming King
You are everything
And still more awesome than I know

More than all I want
More than all I need
You are more than enough for me
More than all I know
More than all I can say
You are more than enough for me [83]

How can you depend on Jesus today? Do you need comfort? Courage? Provision? Health? Hope? Have you believed in Him for eternal life?

*The real miracle in the feeding of the 5000 was that **everyone** ate **all** that they wanted and **all** were **completely** satisfied. There were leftovers – remember?! Let Him completely satisfy you, and those around you will see you feasting at a banquet that they can attend too.*

# Unit Seven  Matthew 14:22 — 17:13

# JESUS WALKS ON WATER

*Ahoy there mate! Permission to come aboard granted. It's time to put out to sea. What an exciting lesson we have today!*

Please pray that the Holy Spirit would teach you
today so that you may walk worthy of the Lord.

Remember the setting from your readings in our last lesson. What time of day was it when the 5000 feasted on bread and fish? See Matthew 14:15.

Please read what happened immediately after the banquet: **Matthew 14:22-33.**

What do you learn about Jesus from this passage?

What do you learn about the disciples from this passage?

What do you learn about Peter from this passage?

*What did Matthew want his readers to learn from this event? It wasn't just a good ole' sailor's tale. Do you remember anyone in the Old Testament walking on water? Noah? There's lots of water in his story, but he needed an ark. Moses? He floated on the Nile as a babe in a basket, and split the sea with his staff but didn't get his feet wet. How about Elisha? He made an iron axhead float, but he all he could do was tread water.*

What does the Old Testament tell us about who is able to walk on the waters?

**Genesis 1:1-2**

**Job 9:8**

**Job 38:16**

**Psalm 77:13-14, 19**

**Psalm 93:3-4**

*God. And God alone. Even though the disciples probably didn't realize it at the moment – Jesus identified Himself to them as: God. The Great I Am. Matthew, Mark and John each record this event with varying details, but the words of Jesus are the same: "It is I." This is literally "ego eimi," "I am." This is the exact phrasing in the Greek translation of the Hebrew "I AM THAT I AM" found in Exodus 3:14.*

What is happening in Exodus 3:13-14?

*And what is happening in Matthew 14:22-33? Matthew is doing more than telling a fascinating "ghost" story. He's preparing us for the most important moment in Peter's life, and anyone else's for that matter – when he recognizes who Jesus actually is! So far, the disciples are following Him, the crowds are amazed at His teaching, and the Pharisees are disgusted with Him. But no one has totally grasped Who He really is. In Chapter 16, we'll see the climatic question: Who do you say that I am?*

> In walking on the water and delivering the disciples from the storm, Jesus exercises divine attributes and accomplishes feats that are the prerogative of God alone. [84]

According to Matthew 14:28-32, when Jesus shows up, Peter takes a leap of faith. Good for him! But what goes wrong? What did Peter do and what was Jesus' rebuke?

*Jesus doesn't miss any opportunity to strengthen His disciples for the ministries they'll have in the future. There's a process going on here. The disciples are learning just Who Jesus is and how they are to respond to Him. They are growing in their faith which will affect their feet! This is true for us as well. When you know Who Jesus is and you trust in the power of God, you can obey His commands – no matter what the weather is.*

*Why doubt? There is no reason at all!*

It's your turn, of course. What is Jesus commanding you to do today?

What is the wonderful conclusion to this event? Read Matthew 14:32-33.

*This is the first time that the disciples address Jesus with this full title. There is joyful worship and amazement at who Jesus is! They've been hearing and seeing the evidence, and they are beginning to believe. Their understanding of Who Christ is will grow deeper and deeper as they spend time with Him, but it won't be until after His resurrection and ascension that they will gain the full comprehension of His identity and deity.*

*Let's rejoice with the disciples in this moment where we have seen that Jesus has all the power of God to walk on the water, to enable Peter to walk on the water, and to save him out of the water. And He has all the power of God to still the storm.*

*I love what happens next.*

What do you learn about the people of Gennesaret from Matthew 14:34-36?

What was Jesus' response to them?

*Jesus fed five thousand in a deserted place, and the people there didn't say a thing. Jesus walked through the wind and waves to the disciples, and they thought He was a ghost. Jesus got out of a boat at Gennesaret – and the people recognized Him!*

*And as many as touched the hem of His robe were made "perfectly well." They were made completely whole. This word hints at salvation for those who demonstrated faith.*

How well do you know Jesus? How would you describe Him to someone who had never heard of Him?

*My prayer for us all comes from Paul's prayer in Ephesians 1:17-19. I pray that the God of our Lord Jesus Christ, the Father of glory, may give to us a spirit of wisdom and of revelation in the knowledge of Him. I pray that the eyes of our hearts may be enlightened, so that we will know the hope of His calling, the riches of the glory of His inheritance in the saints, and the surpassing greatness of His power toward us who believe.*

> In demonstrating His mastery over wind and waves, Jesus clearly is exercising prerogatives previously reserved for Yahweh Himself. [85]

Lesson Two: Matthew 15:1-20

# JESUS OFFENDS THE PHARISEES

*Are you ready for another encounter with the scribes and Pharisees? They will keep showing up with tests and traps for Jesus until they think they have come out as the winners. I'm so glad we know the end of the story. In today's lesson, we'll see that the Pharisee's pop quiz for Jesus doesn't surprise Him, but instead leaves them with a failing grade.*

Please pray that the Holy Spirit will give you a desire to know Jesus more intimately.

Please read Matthew 15:1-20.

Let's get an overview of the speakers and audience in this passage and briefly summarize the questions and comments made.

| VERSE | SPEAKER(S) | AUDIENCE | COMMENTS |
|---|---|---|---|
| Matthew 15:1-2 | | | |
| Matthew 15:3-9 | | | |
| Matthew 15:10-11 | | | |
| Matthew 15:12 | | | |
| Matthew 15:13-14 | | | |
| Matthew 15:15 | | | |
| Matthew 15:16-20 | | | |

148

*I hope that you can see from this perspective that these sixteen verses all fit together and relate to each other. This overview also shows us that the disciples and a crowd were watching and waiting for Jesus' response to the Pharisees.*

How does Mark 7:1-5 describe the Pharisees practice of washing their hands? Why do they do it?

Let's look more closely at what Jesus emphasizes at being crucial. What is being compared in the following verses?

NIV **Matthew 15:3** Jesus replied, "And why do you break the _____  ____ _____ for the sake of _____  _____ ?

NIV **Matthew 15:6** "Thus you nullify the _____  ___  _____ for the sake of _____ _____.

> Jesus was referring to a practice whereby people would dedicate their possessions to God so that they could use their finances for themselves and not for others. For example, if parents needed money, the children could excuse themselves from helping because their resources were already "dedicated" to God. This ruse kept people from honoring their parents by taking care of them in their old age. [86]

*The questions and answers in this passage, while on the surface seem to be about rituals and defilement, are more about the heart than the hands.*

How is the heart of the Pharisees described in Matthew 15:8-9?

How is the heart of man described in Matthew 15:17-20?

*The evidence of a distant and defiled heart is that the commandment of God is ignored. Replaced. Forgotten. Broken. Despised. This is the state of depravity into which all men and women are born. It is totally discouraging, isn't it? I'm surprised that there was no further response from the disciples.*

Our hearts need attention. What does the Psalm 51:10 encourage us to pray for and pursue?

Please turn back to page 43. Summarize what we learned would be a characteristic of a citizen of the kingdom of heaven according to Matthew 5:8.

What does the evidence show about your heart? Are you listening to the words of God or the words of man? Are you following God's commands or your own traditions?

*Please be careful that you do not trust your eternity to traditions or rituals or religion. Going to church, being baptized, taking communion, and celebrating Christmas does not make you a Christian.*

What is the first thing we need in order to be Christians? A new heart. – What is the sacrifice God asks us to bring to Him? A broken and contrite heart. – What is the true circumcision? The circumcision of the heart. – What is genuine obedience? To obey from the heart. – What is saving faith? To believe with the heart. – Where ought Christ to dwell? To dwell in our hearts by faith. – What is the chief request that Wisdom makes to every one? "My son, give me thine heart." [87]

Lesson Three: Matthew 15:21-16:12

# JESUS FEEDS FOUR THOUSAND

*I just realized that Matthew 15 has a strange common denominator in each of its events. Bread. It's not that Jesus is teaching about bread, but comments about bread become the catalyst for His teaching and actions (Matthew 15:2, 26-27, 33).*

May the Word of the Lord today help us draw closer in love and loyalty to Him. Pray that it will.

**Please read Matthew 15:21-28.**

According to verses 21-25, who was the woman, what was her situation and what did she do about it?

According to verses 23-26, how did Jesus respond?


*Does this shock you? It surprises me every time I read it. The disciples seemed to be irritated with this poor woman. And did Jesus call that woman a "little dog"? But don't judge Jesus. He knew what He was doing.*

Then she said (verse 27):


And then He said (verse 28):


> The language describing Gentiles is offensive to modern sensibilities even if the word Jesus uses implies the affection one might have for a house pet. The point here is the redemptive-historical priority of Israel. Jews come first in Jesus' ministry, yet He can be compassionate to Gentiles once the "children" have been fed. His blunt language reflects His culture, yet His commendation of the woman's faith and His upcoming Gentile mission transcend that culture.[88]

How did the woman address Jesus each time she spoke to Him?


How do you respond to the Lord when you don't get the answer you want from Him?


*No matter what His answer is, press on. Worship Him. Walk by faith. That's what He's looking for.*

**Please read Matthew 15:29-31.**

Where was Jesus when He healed the lame, blind, mute, maimed, and many others? Was He healing Jews or Gentiles?


How did the people respond?


*Some commentators think that Jesus was in Gentile territory and that the Gentiles "praised the God of Israel." On the other hand, other commentators point out that Matthew makes absolutely no mention of Gentiles being in the crowd, and that if there were, then he would have made that clear. These commentators also point out that it was appropriate for the people of Israel to praise the God of Israel.*

*What difference does it make? If Jesus was healing Jews, which I think He was, then it's a continuation of the emphasis that He was sent to Israel as her Messiah. He demonstrated His identity and authority. And even though they enjoyed His healing power and generous provision, they did not recognize Him.*

*What happened next?*

**Please read Matthew 15:32-39.**

What is the most interesting thing to you about the feeding of the four thousand?

*Once again, commentators are divided regarding to whom Jesus was ministering. Was it Jews or Gentiles? And commentators also disagree as to whether this was a second version of just one miracle meal. Here is Donald Hagner's comment:*

> We have here variant versions describing what was originally but one event. What inclines one to this conclusion more than anything else is the extreme improbability that after experiencing the feeding of the five thousand and now being confronted with an almost identical situation with seven loaves of bread and a few small fish in their baskets, the disciples should ask, "Where are we to get bread enough in the desert to feed so great a crowd?" [89]

*Now, I know that I'm not as smart as this commentator. But, I believe that God's Word is accurate and intentional. Matthew was a tax collector, a record keeper, and a precise man. His writing has been wonderfully woven together under the direction of the Holy Spirit. So, I must respectfully disagree with the perspective above.*

*We must remember that Jesus takes every opportunity to test and train His disciples.*

What was the disciples' attitude toward the two hungry crowds and the Canaanite woman according to Matthew 14:15, 15:23 and 33?

*You've seen that despite their comments, Jesus fed the people and healed the woman's daughter. Please read one more passage of Scripture while we are considering all these things.*

**Read Matthew 16:1-12.**

How does Jesus rebuke the disciples in this passage?

*Here's what a commentator that I agree with says:*

> The second miracle meal emphasizes such lessons as the compassion of Jesus, His power to do great things with meager resources, and the foreshadowing of the eschatological feast with Jesus. On the basis of these two miracle stories, another lesson will be taught in Matt. 16:5-11, where the disciples' "little faith" will once again be confronted with their preoccupation with physical needs instead of kingdom truth and priorities. In each of the main sections of Matt. 15, Jesus addresses the genuine but flawed faith of the disciples. [90]

*I have acted just like the disciples again and again and again. You probably have too. What were they thinking? What were they __not__ thinking?! That's the problem. We forget Who our Lord is. We forget who we are. We forget that all we have to do is trust Him to "give us our daily bread."*

Has Jesus put anyone in your life to whom you can show His compassion?

What physical needs do you need to entrust to Jesus?

*There's one more thing that I want to tell you about the "miracle meals." It was mentioned in the commentary above and vaguely referred to when we looked at the feeding of the five thousand. These feasts are both a fulfillment of prophecy and an anticipation of the ultimate Messianic banquet in the end times. When Jesus returns and reigns on earth, He will satisfy all the needs of God's people. Isaiah tells us so:*

On this mountain the LORD Almighty will prepare a feast of rich food for all peoples, a banquet of aged wine – the best of meats and the finest of wines. On this mountain He will destroy the shroud that enfolds all peoples, the sheet that covers all nations; He will swallow up death forever. The Sovereign LORD will wipe away the tears from all faces; He will remove the disgrace of His people from all the earth. The LORD has spoken. In that day they will say, "Surely this is our God; we trusted in Him, and He saved us. This is the LORD, we trusted in Him; let us rejoice and be glad in His salvation." Isaiah 25:6-9 [NIV]

*That's going to be one fantastic feast! I'll see you there!*

Lesson Four : Matthew 16

# JESUS ASKS A QUESTION

*Red sky at night, sailors' delight – red sky in the morning, sailors take warning. I just love it that so many of our concepts are based on or verified by Scripture. Way back in 30AD, the people watched the weather to make their plans for the next day.*

*We skimmed over the weather-related passage in our previous lesson. We'll take a quick look at it today too, as we prepare to study the most important discussion in Matthew so far.*

> Please pray for the Holy Spirit to give you wisdom
> to understand that Jesus is the Messiah.

**Based on Matthew 16:1-4,** answer the following questions.

Why did the Pharisees and Sadducees approach Jesus?

> A "sign from heaven" would evidently be something so spectacular and undeniable that it would be clear that it had come from heaven. In this understanding, "heaven" probably stands for God. [91]

Jesus pointed out their competency in meteorology and their incompetence in what?

*If there had been TV and Internet back then, the feeding of thousands with just a few loaves of bread and a few pieces of fish would have made the headlines. And Jesus did that more than once! The Pharisees and Sadducees had enough of a network to know what Jesus was doing. They even saw some of His miracles themselves. For them however, seeing was not believing.*

*So, Jesus ended the discussion and walked away.*

What did Jesus warn the disciples about, according to Matthew 16:5-12?

*These two groups of religious leaders did not normally associate with each other. They had doctrinal differences. The Pharisees adhered strictly to the oral interpretations of the Scriptures and to their ancestral traditions. The Sadducees did not believe in life after death, or the resurrection of the body, or in future punishment as part of judgment. However, the two groups did share one thing in common: because they did not believe the signs of the times, they did not believe that Jesus was the Messiah.*

*It was a critical time for the disciples to beware of them. It was a critical time for the disciples to believe in Jesus as the Messiah, to believe in the Scriptures, and to believe in the resurrection.*

**Please read Matthew 16:13-21.**

*It's time for the question of the ages: Who is Jesus?*

Who did Jesus say that He was?

Who did "some" say that He was?


*We've been considering this question throughout Matthew! The people have been asking, wondering, watching, waiting – for Jesus to say it Himself.*

What were the questions asked in the verses below?

**Matthew 8:27**

**Matthew 11:2**

**Matthew 12:23**

Who did Peter say that He was?

> …now in a private, peaceful, meditative setting, Jesus for the first time elicits from the disciples, represented by Peter, the reasoned and careful conclusion that He is indeed the Christ, the Messiah of promise. [92]

*There is nothing more important about Jesus than the fact that He is the Christ. The Messiah. The Son of God. It's what we learned about Him in our very first lessons. Please turn back to pages 11-12 and 16-17, and review your notes ,then answer the next question.*

What does "Christ" mean? And why was there an expectation of His coming?


*Let's rejoice in this moment with Peter and the disciples! They have seen and they have believed. The evidence that Jesus, the Son of Man, is the Christ – the Son of the living God, is undeniable! So Peter boldly confesses and humbly worships as he says, "You are the Christ." And yet, Jesus makes it absolutely clear that Peter did not come to this conclusion by his own intelligence.*

**Look back at Matthew 16:13-21.**

How did Peter understand Jesus' identity?


What were the results of Peter's confession?

*Knowing who Jesus is – is life changing! It brings blessing. Purpose. Authority. Sacrifice.*

*We'll consider this passage further in our next lesson. For now, think about this: are you enjoying the blessing of knowing Jesus, the Christ?*

How does knowing Jesus make you happy?

Lesson Five: Matthew 16:16-23

# JESUS BUILDS HIS CHURCH

*Matthew 16:18 has been described as "among the most controversial in all of Scripture."* [93] *Oh, great. You know, it shouldn't be surprising. The most important question of all time (Matthew 16:15), followed by the most important declaration of all time (Matthew 16:16), followed by the most important resolution of all time (Matthew 16:21) surely become the targets of spiritual opposition. We wrestle with spiritual wickedness in high places.*

*We'll take a little time to try to sort things out. But, please do be careful not to get bogged down in the slightly less important things. Keep your eyes on Jesus!*

Ask for the Lord to give you
discernment regarding today's Scriptures.

*Names are very important in Matthew 16:13-20. Jesus, and therefore Matthew, used a little wordplay to make their point. We've got to look at the words they used.*

Please look up the definition for the following words:
**Peter: Strong's #4074**
**Greek word:**
**Greek definition:**


**Rock: Strong's #4073**
**Greek word:**
**Greek definition:**

Underline or highlight the pronouns: *you* and *I*, as well as the names in Matthew 16:15-19:

He said to them, "But who do you say that I am?" [16] Simon Peter answered and said, "You are the Christ, the Son of the living God." [17] Jesus answered and said to him, "Blessed are you, Simon Bar-Jonah, for flesh and blood has not revealed this to you, but My Father who is in heaven. [18] And I also say to you that you are Peter, and on this rock I will build My church, and the gates of Hades shall not prevail against it. [19] And I will give you the keys of the kingdom of heaven, and whatever you bind on earth will be bound in heaven, and whatever you loose on earth will be loosed in heaven." NKJ

> Jesus is speaking of Peter in 16:18 just as clearly as Peter is speaking of Jesus in 16:16. [94]

*Is Peter the rock, the foundation, upon which Jesus says that He will build His church? Based on the pronouns above, yes. But don't forget that all the disciples were there. And Jesus had said to them, "who do you say that I am?" Peter spoke for and represented the group of disciples.*

What do Ephesians 2:20 and Revelation 21:14 tell us?

*Because the disciples knew that Jesus was the Christ, they were the ones commissioned to share this news with the world. Peter was definitely a leader, and he is described best as "first among equals." What Peter would proclaim for the rest of his life was that Jesus was the Christ, the Son of the living God, the One Who came to give His life as a sacrifice for our sins. That's the most important thing we can learn from Matthew 16:13-23.*

*The "gates of hell" (the power of death) have no power over those who are saved by God's grace through Christ (Ephesians 2:5). And the "keys of the kingdom" (authority) are given to those who follow Jesus. This is authority to do on earth what God in heaven wills should be done. (That's a brief summary of Matthew 16:19!)*

> The church does not get man's will done in heaven; it obeys God's will on earth. [95]

*You've probably still got questions. But let's stay focused on Jesus' mission.*

What was Jesus' pre-ordained determination, according to Matthew 16:21?

When does this verse say that Jesus talked about His purpose and with whom did He discuss it?

Note major events of Jesus' life on the timeline below that you can remember up to this point. The last mark should be Peter's confession.

*"From that time..." is a very important phrase. Matthew used it in 4:17 to introduce Jesus' ministry. Now he uses it to bring us to the second main stage of the gospel which will focus on the death of Christ. Everything is going to change. Peter doesn't like the plan.*

What extreme action does Peter take in Matthew 16:22-23?

What does 1 Corinthians 1:23 tell you about the death of Christ?

*Peter had just said, "You are the Messiah!" and with that declaration, Peter and the disciples expected the glorious reign of the Promised One. How could the Messiah be killed? The disciples were growing in their understanding of Jesus' identity, but it was far from complete.*

> In Matthew 16:23, Jesus speaks to Peter addressing him as Satan; it is as though Peter's response were inspired by Satan. Jesus' rebuke, "get behind me, Satan," is thus almost exactly the same as that of Matthew 4:10. The command in Greek is identical. [96]

How did Jesus explain Peter's attitude? What was the problem?

Let's stop right there and think about how we are just like Peter so many times. What's on your mind today? The things of God or the things of men?

*Jesus turned a moment of man into an opportunity for a message from God. We don't know how Peter responded to Jesus' rebuke, but we do know how Jesus instructed him and the rest of the disciples. Not only must Jesus be willing to suffer and die, but His disciples must as well.*

Please read the entire account of this turning point in Jesus' and the disciples' lives: Matthew 16:13-28.

Jesus told Peter and the disciples how to keep their minds on the things of God. What was His clear command in Matthew 16:24?

This is not the first time that Jesus has taught these concepts. We spent time studying them in our lessons on Matthew 10:32-39. Please review your notes on pages 106-108. What does it mean to take up your cross?

Please look up the definition for the following word:
**Deny: Strong's #533**
**Greek word:**
**Greek definition:**

*Matthew uses the Greek 3rd person imperative which has been translated as "let him deny himself." The imperative places a requirement on an individual. We don't have an equivalent in English to the Greek 3rd person imperative, but it would best be understood as the strong command: "He must deny himself."*

What were the three reasons that Jesus gave for denying self, taking up our cross, and following Him? (The Greek uses the word "for" at the beginning of verse 25, verse 26, and verse 27.)

Deny yourself. Say no to the things of *self* and the things of *man.* What do you need to deny?

Take up your cross. Say yes to the things of *God* and the things of *suffering.* What do you need to embrace?

*Follow Jesus. Do you realize that your decisions will affect more than the next 24 hours? They will affect more than the next 24 years. Your decisions will affect eternity.*

## JESUS SHINES LIKE THE SUN

*"I'm going to die." These were the alarming words that the disciples heard from Jesus. And they fixated on those words alone, apparently forgetting the good news that Jesus also gave them: "I'll be raised on the third day." Peter panicked. But the Lord in His wisdom and grace gave him and two other disciples a glimpse into the realm of unseen spiritual reality.*

*We're about to see a true mountain-top experience.*

Ask for the Spirit to open your eyes
to see the glory of the Lord.

**Please read Matthew 17:1-9.**

*I prefer for you to read the passages in your own Bible, but I want you to see how Matthew emphasized things in the Greek. I've added italic type, underlining, capital letters and exclamations to help you see what the Greek communicates.*

**Matthew 17:1-9** *And* six days later Jesus took with Him Peter and James and John his brother, and brought them up to a high mountain by themselves.

² *And* He was transfigured before them;

*and* His face shone like the sun,

*and* His garments became as white as light.

³ *And* BEHOLD! Moses and Elijah appeared to them, talking with Him.

⁴ *And* Peter answered and said to Jesus, "Lord, it is good for us to be here; if You wish, I will make three tabernacles here, one for You, and one for Moses, and one for Elijah."

⁵ While he was still speaking, BEHOLD! a bright cloud overshadowed them;

*and* BEHOLD! a voice out of the cloud, saying, "This is My beloved Son, with whom I am well-pleased; listen to Him!"

⁶ *And* when the disciples heard this, they fell on their faces and were much afraid.

⁷ *And* Jesus came to them and touched them and said, "Arise, and do not be afraid."

⁸ *And* lifting up their eyes, they saw no one, except Jesus *Himself* alone.

⁹ *And* as they were coming down from the mountain, Jesus commanded them, saying, "Tell the vision to no one until the Son of Man has risen from the dead."

What supernatural events happened up on the mountain?

How did Mark and Luke describe what happened to Jesus? See Mark 9:3 and Luke 9:29.


What do the following verses tell you about God?
**Psalm 104:2**


**Daniel 7:9**


What do the following verses tell you about Jesus?
**Colossians 2:9**


**Hebrews 1:1-3**


What was Peter's eyewitness testimony about the transfiguration in 2 Peter 1:16-18?


Using three different colors, in the passage on the previous page, highlight the statements that describe: (1) Jesus, (2) Moses and Elijah, (3) God.

Who is featured prominently in this passage?

What is the one command given and who gave it?

*I'm going to ask you two questions. Consider the context of the passage and what we've learned about Jesus from Matthew.*

Why do you think that the transfiguration of Jesus followed Peter's declaration of His identity and His own announcement about His death and resurrection?


Why do you think Jesus told Peter, James, and John not to tell anyone about their vision?


*I have to admit that I'm surprised that Jesus didn't allow all the disciples to see His glory. He didn't even allow them to hear about it from the three who did. It was an "eyes only" event – only Peter, James, and John were on the "need to know" list. They joined Moses, Isaiah, Ezekiel and Daniel, who also had been given glimpses of the glory of God.*

*Do you realize that there is no longer a short list of those who are privileged to see the radiance of the divine glory? Jesus shines through all the Scriptures. If you've been saved by grace through faith, you just have to open your eyes and ears to see and hear Him there.*

You don't have to climb a mountain to see Jesus in His glory. Where do you like to read your Bible? When do you like to read your Bible? With whom do you like to read your Bible?

*Well, let's keep reading it…so that we can see more of Jesus.*

**Please read Matthew 17:9-13.**

*Jesus, Peter, James, and John were coming down the mountain, talking about what they had just experienced.*

What did the disciples want to know?

What do you learn from Malachi 3:1 and 4:5-6?

> The three disciples evidently did not comprehend the reference to Christ's death in v. 9. The problem they raised concerned the transfiguration. They had just seen Elijah on the mountain. If the scribes were correct that Elijah must come before the kingdom would arrive, why should the disciples not inform everyone that Elijah had appeared on the mountain? The Lord informed His three apostles that the scribes were right in their interpretation of Malachi 3:1; 4:5-6. The fact that Christ used the phrase "will restore all things" indicates that the prophecy still has a future fulfillment. [97]

*While the disciples were eager to say that they had seen Elijah, Jesus turned the conversation to more important matters in Matthew 17:12.*

What parallel does Jesus draw between the Elijah who had come already (John the Baptist) and the Son of Man?

*Jesus was preparing His disciples for the events to come. But it wasn't time yet. There was still much to do. The multitudes were waiting at the bottom of the mountain. The disciples, a dad, and a demon-possessed son needed Jesus. We'll climb down the mountain now and meet them in our next lesson.*

# Unit Eight    Matthew 17:14—19:30

# JESUS CALLS FOR FAITH AND A FISH

Pray that the Spirit will strengthen
your faith through your study today.

**Please read Matthew 17:14-27.**

What had happened while Jesus was on the mountain?

How does Jesus handle the situation?

What had Jesus commissioned the disciples to do in Matthew 10:7?

*Jesus has been predicting His death and resurrection. He knows that He will also ascend to heaven, leaving the disciples to continue His ministry. They had great success on their first independent missionary journey. But now they're having trouble.*

What did Jesus say about the multitude in verse 17?

Please look up the definition for the following word:
**Faithless: Strong's #571**
**Greek word:**
**Greek definition:**

> "Unbelieving" indicates that the current generation has not as a whole placed their faith in Jesus as the anticipated Messiah; "perverse" indicates that they have become distorted in their evaluation of Jesus. [98]

How did Jesus answer the disciples' question in verses 19-21?

Please look up the definition for the following words:

**Unbelief (also translated as "little faith"): Strong's #3640**

**Greek word:**

**Greek definition:**


**Faith: Strong's #4102**

**Greek word:**

**Greek definition:**


*We know that the disciples do have faith in Jesus as the Christ – the Messiah of God. Peter had just made that declaration, as the spokesperson for all the disciples. But they have a problem that keeps coming up – little faith. (See Matthew 8:26, 14:31, 16:8.)*

*The disciples had weak faith. Their confidence was shaken by the unbelief of the multitudes. But that was no excuse, and Jesus rebuked them for their weak, unproductive faith. He wanted their faith to grow, like a mustard seed – remember how large a tree it becomes (Matthew 13:32)?*

*Jesus encouraged the disciples by telling them that as little as their faith was right now, when it grew, through practice and trusting Him (through prayer) – it would be able to move mountains! They had faith. It was just in seed form. And that seed would grow. And they would be able to accomplish whatever Jesus commanded of them. There was hope!*

We can be negatively influenced by those around us, just as it seems that the disciples were. What does Hebrews 12:1-3 tell us to do?


By the way, what's the connection between faith, and prayer and fasting?


*I started out studying this passage with bewilderment. I just didn't get it. The disciples may have felt that way too! But Jesus has encouraged me, just as He did the disciples, to grow in faith and keep my eyes on Him. There are mountains that are going to move! "Moving a mountain is proverbial in Jewish literature for doing what is virtually impossible."* [99]

We need that empowerment especially when we know that there are extreme challenges ahead. The disciples would soon face ministry without the physical, visible presence of Jesus. What does Jesus emphasize in the following verses? Note the specific detail He gives.

**Matthew 16:21**


**Matthew 17:9**

**Matthew 17:12**


**Matthew 17:22-23**


*The comment that the disciples were exceedingly sorrowful indicates that they were beginning to accept the reality that Jesus was going to die. But it also suggests that they did not yet grasp the impact of His resurrection. Jesus would keep teaching them until they had heard everything they needed to know.*

*Matthew now tells us what many scholars consider to be a "fish tale"! Both financiers and fishermen will find this account intriguing!*

If you were a newscaster, you'd want to get this story straight. What would you report, based on Matthew 17:24-27?



What do the following phrases teach you about Jesus?
Verse 25 - "Jesus anticipated him…"


Verse 26 - "Then the sons are free…"


Verse 27 - "lest we offend them…"


Verse 27 - "give it to them for Me and you…"


*Jesus, who had every right to be excused from the Temple tax, paid it Himself, so that no one else would be tempted to disobey the law. He modeled humility for Peter's sake. Paul explained that he followed the same principle regarding food and drink in Romans 14:13-21.*

What is the key attitude to have, according to Romans 14:13 and 21?


What are you free to do that might cause someone else to stumble into sin?


*Do unto others as you would have them do unto you. Do nothing out of selfish ambition or vain conceit, but in humility consider others better than yourselves. Each of you should look not only to your own interests, but also to the interests of others. Your attitude should be the same as that of Christ Jesus. (Matthew 7:12, Philippians 2:3-5) This is what the next sermon is all about. Humility. Putting others first.*

# JESUS HUMBLES HIS DISCIPLES

*Do you consider yourself successful? What are your accomplishments? Have you achieved greatness? Are you strong, independent, and think you can do anything? Give it up. Give it all up. Humility and complete dependence on the Lord are the basic characteristics of Jesus' disciples. This is what Jesus explains and illustrates in His fourth sermon in Matthew. We've studied the Sermon on the Mount (Matthew 5 – 7), the Commissioning of the Twelve (Matthew 10), the Kingdom Parables (Matthew 13), and now it's time for the Humility of the Believer.*

Invite the Holy Spirit to lead, direct, teach and
counsel you though the Word of the Lord today.

**According to Matthew 18:1-4:**

What prompted this sermon?

What is Jesus' visual aid?

What is His statement?

> In the ancient world, children were valued primarily for the benefit that they brought to the family by enhancing the workforce, adding to the defensive power, and guaranteeing the future glory of the house. But they had no rights or significance apart from their future value to the family and were powerless in society. The humility of a child consists of the inability to advance his or her own cause apart from the help and resources of a parent. The child can really do nothing for himself and will die if left alone. [100]

Based on the description of children above, what was it about them that made them an example for His disciples?

*It's not so much that we are to **act** like a child, as we are to have the **status** and **dependence** of a child. Now, the next thing that I have to tell you will probably surprise you as much as it surprised me. Throughout the rest of Matthew 18, when Jesus refers to children, He is referring to His disciples – those who believe in Him as the Messiah.*

**Please read Matthew 18:1-14.**

Verses 5 and 6 present a contrast – what is it?

Please look up the definition for the following words:
**Receive: Strong's #1209**
**Greek word:**
**Greek definition:**


**Stumble: Strong's #4624**
**Greek word:**
**Greek definition:**


*Reminder: Taking offense, literally, "stumbling" (Greek: scandalizo), refers to a serious loss of faith, spiritual defeat, or apostasy.* [101]

Please read Matthew 18:5-6 again. Based on your understanding of the example of the child, and the Greek word definitions, how would you explain these verses?


*Jesus teaches the disciples that they are so valuable to Him that the worst thing someone could do to them would be to cause them to sin. Our treatment of other believers is critical. Woe to the one who causes another believer to sin. Once again, Jesus makes radical demands on His disciples. We might prompt a brother or sister to stumble into sin, or we might allow ourselves to stumble into sin. Don't do it!*

What are the eternal options that Jesus presents in verses 8-9?


Have you ever, or do you need to now, cut off or cut out, anything that causes you to sin? This is obviously metaphorically speaking!


*Jesus continues His sermon with an emphasis on the childlikeness of the believer. He refers to disciples again as "little ones."*

What is main point of Matthew 18:10-14?


Jesus loves the little children,  all the children of the world,

red and yellow, black and white,  they are precious in His sight,

Jesus loves the little children of the world.

*As far as I know, this song has always applied to little children, literally. But, based on the teaching of Matthew 18:1-14, I'd like to apply it to **all** God's children – whatever our age! I am precious in His sight. You are precious in His sight — so much so that He makes His angels minister to us.*

What do angels do for believers, according to the following verses?
**Psalm 34:7**


**Psalm 91:11-12**


**Hebrews 1:14**


*We've been looking at a critical passage for our relationship with fellow believers. It's taken a lot of study for it to start to sink in for me. Please read through Matthew 18:1-14 once again.*

Who cares about who's the greatest now? Do you have any attitudes toward other believers, generally or specifically, that need to be confessed and repented? Has this passage caused you to consider how you treat your brothers and sisters in Christ?




*God the Father does not want any believer to stumble in sin, so why wouldn't we share that same conviction? If we care about what God cares about, then we will be careful not to lead them astray.*

**Please read Matthew 18:15-35.**

*Family dynamics. How do you treat your brothers and sisters in your home? How do you treat your brothers and sisters in the church? Jesus' sermon on the "humility of the believer" continues in the second half of Chapter 18.*

Outline this passage of Scripture. You should have at least three sections.




*I hope today's lesson has helped you see the continuity of thought in Matthew 18. The following comment regarding Matthew 18:15-17 will remind us about the lessons in the first half of Chapter 18, which show us why the second half is so important:*

The procedure spelled out here will be necessary, since Jesus has just taught that offenses are inevitable (Matthew 18:7). The Father's total dedication to His little ones dictates that offenses within the community (body of Christ) be dealt with promptly and fairly. [102]

*We'll consider how to confront a sinning member of the family of God in our next lesson. Let's end this lesson with a summary.*

How are we to treat each other in the family of God?

Lesson Three:  Matthew 18:15-35

# JESUS DEALS WITH DISCIPLINE

*Let's look closely at the four steps that Jesus explains we should take when confronting a sinning believer.*

Pray that you will be open to the counsel and conviction of the Holy Spirit today.

Note the action to be taken in the following steps.

Matthew 18:15 - Step One: Personal Confrontation

Matthew 18:16 – Step Two: Peer Confrontation

Matthew 18:17a – Step Three: Community Confrontation

Matthew 18:17b – Step Four: Community Rejection

*These steps are often referred to as "church discipline." These steps should be followed by the pastors and leaders of churches when those members in their congregations are caught up in sin. But you see that it begins with one person. Believers have a responsibility to the Lord to hold each other accountable.*

170

*You might be thinking: "judge not; let him who is without sin cast the first stone." But in Matthew 18, Jesus wasn't talking about condemning someone. He was talking about restoring someone to fellowship with God and man. This doesn't mean that you roam the halls of the church like a policeman looking for someone speeding one mile over the limit. If you are aware of a believer who is continuing in unconfessed and unaddressed sin, then you are commanded by Jesus to reprove him.*

Please look up the following word:
**Reprove: Strong's #1651**
**Greek word:**
**Greek definition:**

Why must a sinner be reproved, according to the following verses?
**John 3:20**

**Ephesians 5:11, 13**

**1 Timothy 5:20**

How does Galatians 5:26-6:1 tell us to approach a sinning believer?

Will you commit yourself to obedience to Jesus' command – to go to a believer who continues in sin – and expose that sin? Please write a prayer of dedication, requesting wisdom, discernment, and humility in these situations.

*Following the steps of restoration (or rejection, if necessary), Jesus summarizes His comments and gives authority to the church. Matthew 18:18-19 are two verses that have been interpreted in a variety of ways. This is where the Roman Catholic church derives its authority to forgive sins. Verse 19 is the basis for some who "name it and claim it" from God, expecting to receive anything that they want.* [103]

**Please read Matthew 18:15-22.** We've got to remember the context of verses 18-19.

What assurance does Jesus give the disciples in Matthew 18:18-19?

Please look up the definition for the following words:

**Bind: Strong's #1210**
**Greek word:**
**Greek definition:**


**Loose: Strong's #3089**
**Greek word:**
**Greek definition:**


> If a person has received Jesus Christ as Savior and Lord, the church can tell him with perfect confidence that his sins are loosed, that is, forgiven, because he has met God's condition for forgiveness, namely, trust in His Son. If on the other hand, a person refuses to receive Christ as Savior and acknowledge Him as Lord, the church can tell him with equal confidence that his sins are bound, that is, not forgiven, because he has not met God's condition for forgiveness. [104]

*Let's think about Matthew 18:20 for a minute. Do we have to have two or three believers gathered together for Jesus to be with us? I'm expecting you to say "no". Let's learn to quote verse 20 at the appropriate times – when the church is gathered together to restore a sinning believer.*

*And let's learn to quote scriptures that guarantee the presence of the Lord in our midst:*

**Hebrews 13:5:** He Himself has said, "I will never desert you, nor will I ever forsake you." NAS

For now, would you examine your own heart? And pray for conviction of sin, so that you won't be bound up in it or have to face the steps of church discipline.



**1 John 1:6-9** If we confess our sins, he is faithful and just and will forgive us our sins and purify us from all unrighteousness. NIV

*Jesus loves the little children. That's us, remember? We are precious in His sight. We are not to cause each other to stumble into sin, and we are to forgive our fellow believers who sin against us. But how many times? The rabbis taught that 3 times was enough. So Peter was pretty generous when he asked Jesus about forgiving others.*

According to Matthew 18:21-22, how many times did Peter suggest that someone be forgiven? How many times did Jesus say to do it? (Do the math in the NAS and NKJ– be specific.)

Would you keep a record of that many occasions of forgiveness? What was Jesus' point?

*Forgive others, because God has forgiven you. How much? More than you even realize. That's one of the key messages of the following parable.*

**Please read Matthew 18:23-35.**

What is the most surprising thing about this parable to you?

*The debits and credits on the spreadsheet were way out of balance. The servant owed "an astonishingly large amount of money – ten thousand talents."* [105]

> **Debt:** 10,000 talents which equals 60 million denarii.(1 talent = 6000 denarii)
> **Daily wages:** 1 denarius / day
> **Days to payoff debt:** 60 million days or 193,000 years (based on 310 workdays/year)

What had the servant said about his debt in Matthew 18:26?

*There is no financial advisor that could show this servant how to get out of his debt! It was impossible. So the king, obviously representing God, showed mercy and forgave the debt he owed but could not pay.*

How much did the fellow slave owe to the one whose debt had been forgiven? How long would it take to pay it back?

How do the 10,000 talent debt and the 100 denarii debt relate to God's forgiveness of us and our forgiveness of other believers?

What was Jesus' warning in Matthew 18:35?

What did Jesus say in Matthew 6:14-15?

*If the King of the Universe forgives you of **all** the sins that you have committed against Him, then you can forgive a fellow believer of his few sins against you. If you can't do that, then you've really got to examine your salvation. Those who have been forgiven will be forgiving. This is the high and holy calling of a citizen of the kingdom of heaven.*

# JESUS GIVES MARRIAGE COUNSELING

Ask the Lord to give you the strength and courage
to embrace His teachings today.

*Jesus not only modeled forgiveness, but He also modeled kindness and compassion.*

How does Matthew 19:1-2 show this?

The travel details in verse 1 are important. Jesus moved from where to where?

*These verses are Matthew's transition from the fourth sermon to the next narrative section in his book. In his commentary on Matthew, David Turner entitles this section "Opposition Comes to a Head in Judea -Matthew 19:1-26:2."*

*It doesn't take long for those opposing Jesus to show up.*

Who comes to Jesus, and why, in Matthew 19:3?

---

The Pharisees' question about divorce was dangerous. John the Baptist's answer had resulted in imprisonment and ultimately execution (14:3-11). The use of the word **testing** indicates malicious intent of the query. [106]

The Pharisees came to test Jesus on a question they had frequently debated among themselves. The issue was not divorce itself, the right to which they took for granted, but rather the justifiable grounds for divorce. Would Jesus side with the school of Rabbi Shammai, which allowed divorce only on the grounds of sexual immorality, or would He side with the school of Rabbi Hillel, which sanctioned divorce on the most trivial grounds? [107]

---

*What would Jesus do? He won't get tangled up in the middle of things. He'll go back to the beginning.*

**Please read Matthew 19:3-10.**

What reasons did Jesus give for married people to remain married? Note the reasons and match them to their sources: Genesis 1:27 and Genesis 2:24.

*"Dearly Beloved, we are gathered together in the sight of God and in the presence of these witnesses to join this man and this woman in holy matrimony." God ordained marriage between one man and one woman. God ordained the separation of a man from his parents, and God ordained the union of man and woman as one. God's plan is a blessing (relationship), it gives purpose (be fruitful and multiply), and it is an illustration of His love and commitment to His people. There is no better place to apply Matthew 18 (forgiving fellow believers) than marriage.*

*Sadly, there are as many divorces in the church as there are outside of the church. And the biblical definition of marriage is no longer viewed as the final word.*

*Let me repeat something that is critically important: God ordained marriage between one man and one woman (Genesis 1:27; 2:24). That is the only definition of marriage. If He had intended for a man to marry a man, or a woman to marry a woman, He would have created and defined marriage that way.*

*After Jesus explained God's plan for marriage, the Pharisees tried to trap Him with another question.*

**Fill in the blanks below:**

Matthew 19:7-8: "They said to Him, 'Why then did Moses _____ to give a certificate of divorce, and to put her away?' He said to them, "Moses, because of the _____ __ ___ _____, _____ you to divorce your wives, but from the _____ it was not so."

*So Moses did not command that a man divorce his wife, and neither did Jesus.*

**According to Matthew 19:9:**

What did Jesus say would happen to a man who divorced his wife and married another woman?


And what would be the situation for a man who married a divorced woman?



*The seventh commandment says: "Thou shalt not commit adultery" Exodus 20:14. The Hebrew word for adultery is "naaph" and it means "sexual intercourse with the wife or betrothed of another man."* [108] *Adultery breaks the "one flesh" union between husband and wife.*

What does Leviticus 20:10 say about adulterers?


*That instruction regarding the consequences of adultery shows the seriousness of the sin. But Jesus didn't stone the woman caught in the act of adultery, because He forgave her. The Biblical view of adultery has always been and will always be—that it is sin.*

*Jesus' statement to the Pharisees indicates that if a man divorced his wife, just because that's what he wanted to do, and then married another woman, he would be committing adultery because in God's eyes that man was still united to his first wife. And if a woman was divorced, just because the man wanted to divorce her, and another man married her, then he too would be committing adultery because in God's eyes that woman was still united to her first husband.*

*The focus has been on a man divorcing his wife, because in the culture of that day, the Jewish man could divorce his wife for almost any reason, while a woman divorcing her husband was almost unheard of and she rarely was granted divorce from her husband even on the most serious grounds.*

*Jesus implied in Matthew 19:9 that one could divorce his wife or her husband if they committed sexual immorality. This is actually a gracious opportunity for the adulterer to be able to repent of their sin. It also allows the innocent husband or wife to remarry without committing adultery themselves.*

What does the prophet say is the Lord's perspective on marriage and divorce in Malachi 2:14-16?

What does Paul teach about marriage in 1 Corinthians 7:2-5; 10-13?

How are the marriage vows to be carried out according to Ephesians 5:22-33?

Please read Matthew 19:3-9, once again, and remember the reasons to remain married, as noted in the previous exercises.

What are your reactions to all of these Scriptures regarding marriage, adultery, and divorce?

*After contemplating all the scenarios regarding marriage and divorce, I can almost understand why the disciples said: "if this is the case, it's better not to marry!" Matthew 19:10 NLT But I am so very thankful for my husband who has shown me the love of Christ since December 27, 1986. (That's 30 years as of 2016!)*

*It is okay not to marry though.*

What does Jesus have to say about celibacy in Matthew 19:11-12?

And what does Paul say about it in 1 Corinthians 7:7-9?


Please turn back to 1 Corinthians 7:32-34. How does Paul describe the ministry of one who is single?


*These verses encourage singles to take advantage of their singleness and serve the Lord with a "single" focus!*

*There are those who are just as Jesus described – single, and celibate, for heaven's sake. Betty was a single woman who taught my college women's Bible study. The most vivid lessons I learned from her were about being a wife and a mother, from our study on Titus 2:3-5! Amy is an amazing servant of the Lord, who, although being single, has "birthed" many children through her ministry with a home for unwed mothers. And Kristin is one precious believer who inspires and trains college women, and who holds her married friends accountable to the Scriptures too. If you are single, you have been given a special gift and responsibility which allows you to serve the Lord with a single focus.*

Do you know a single Christian that you could encourage as they faithfully serve the Lord?

Lesson Five: Matthew 19:13-26

# JESUS WITH THE WEE AND THE WEALTHY

*We've seen Jesus teach about marriage, divorce, remarriage, and singleness. Now it's time to give the children some attention.*

Please pray for your time studying
God's Word today. Then pray for a child.

Please read Matthew 19:13-15 and the parallel account in Mark 10:13-16 on the next page.

**Matthew 19:13-15** [13] Then *some* children were brought to Him so that He might lay His hands on them and pray; and the disciples rebuked them. [14] But Jesus said, "Let the children alone, and do not hinder them from coming to Me; for the kingdom of heaven belongs to such as these." [15] And after laying His hands on them, He departed from there. NAS

**Mark 10:13-16** [13] And they were bringing children to Him so that He might touch them; and the disciples rebuked them. [14] But when Jesus saw this, He was indignant and said to them, "Permit the children to come to Me; do not hinder them; for the kingdom of God belongs to such as these. [15] Truly I say to you, whoever does not receive the kingdom of God like a child shall not enter it at all." [16] And He took them in His arms and began blessing them, laying His hands upon them. NAS

Who brought the children to Jesus and why?

What was the disciples response?

Did the disciples remember their previous lesson regarding "becoming like a little child" (Matthew 18:2-5)? How did Jesus remind them?

*I just wonder... what were they thinking?!?! Well, I quickly forget the lessons that I think I've just learned from the Lord too. Isn't it great that He gives us so many opportunities to practice what we are being taught? Please notice that the kingdom of heaven is still the focus of Jesus' teaching. He continues to tell how to enter in and how to live as a citizen of it.*

What did Jesus actually do with the children?

*Now we can sing the song again. "Jesus loves the little children." Do you? Do you treat children with the kindness and gentleness that Jesus did? Are there children that you are praying for? I know some grandmothers out there are burdened for their grandchildren. What about your neighbors? And your children's friends?*

How can you show Jesus' love and blessing to little children?

*Not only did parents bring their children to Jesus, but a young man brought himself to Him, with a sincere question. How good is good enough?*

**Please read Matthew 19:16-17 in both versions below.**

<u>NKJV:</u> **Matthew 19:16-17** [16] Now behold, one came and said to Him, "Good Teacher, what good thing shall I do that I may have eternal life?" [17] So He said to him, "Why do you call Me good? No one is good but One, that is, God. But if you want to enter into life, keep the commandments."

<u>NAS:</u> **Matthew 19:16-17** [16] And behold, one came to Him and said, "Teacher, what good thing shall I do that I may obtain eternal life?" [17] And He said to him, "Why are you asking Me about what is good? There is only One who is good; but if you wish to enter into life, keep the commandments."

*I love the NKJV, but there is dispute over whether the young man calls Jesus "Good Teacher" or just "Teacher." And there is dispute over Jesus' response to him. After looking at my Greek Bible and other scholars comments, I have to agree with the NAS translation. We'll see that Jesus (and therefore Matthew) makes a subtle point.*

How might Jesus' statement prompt the man to remember Deuteronomy 6:4 (the Shema)?


When Jesus answers this man's question about what good he should do, what does He indicate about Himself?


Describe everything you can from Matthew 19:16-26 about the man who comes to Jesus.


Does he realize that keeping the commandments is good — but not good enough — to gain eternal life? How is that expressed?


Did Jesus give the young man a command that was impossible for him to accomplish? Did he face a "could not" or a "would not" situation?


Note what the commands below actually required of the young man, and which ones actually lead to eternal life.

**Go...**

**Sell...**

**Give...**

**Come...**

**Follow...**

> So attached was he to his great wealth that he was unwilling to part with it. Such is the insidiousness of riches that, as Bengel notes, "If the Lord had said, Thou art rich, and art too fond of thy riches, the young man would have denied it." He had to be confronted with all the force of a radical alternative. [109]

What have you surrendered to follow Jesus? Is there anything that you are holding to that is making you lag behind in radical obedience to Him? Consider material things, emotional baggage, personal goals, and relational desires as well as what others think about you or you think about yourself.

*I hope that Matthew went after that rich young man because he could certainly relate to having wealth.*

*The two passages we've just looked at actually have a few things in common: young children and a young man – come to Jesus. Entrance into the kingdom of heaven is referred to in both passages. Change is required: humility, obedience, and surrender are the marks of a disciple in the kingdom of heaven. The disciples are taking it all in.*

All to Jesus I surrender; Humbly at His feet I bow,
Worldly pleasures all forsaken; Take me Jesus, take me now.

All to Jesus I surrender; Make me, Savior, wholly Thine;
Let me feel the Holy Spirit, Truly know that Thou art mine.

All to Jesus I surrender; Lord, I give myself to Thee;
Fill me with Thy love and power; Let Thy blessing fall on me.

All to Jesus I surrender; Now I feel the sacred flame.
Oh, the joy of full salvation! Glory, glory to His Name! [110]

# JESUS GIVES GOOD NEWS

*Have you heard Tevya's song from Fiddler on the Roof? "If I were a rich man...ya da da da da da da.... All day long I'd di di di da doo... ............." Oh, the dreams of being rich. Oh, what we would do! But oh, how hard it is for a rich man to enter the kingdom of heaven (Matthew 19:23). This well known passage gives us great news. Did you know that?*

*Matthew has juxtaposed little children – of such is the kingdom of heaven, with the rich young ruler seeking eternal life – who went away from Jesus sorrowful because he had many possessions. The future is at stake. Not just tomorrow, but forever. Jesus takes advantage of the teachable moment after the rich young man leaves to emphasize the power of God for salvation.*

Please ask the Holy Spirit to deepen your understanding and thankfulness for salvation.

Please read Matthew 19:13-30. Mark, circle, or highlight: "kingdom of heaven," "eternal life," "enter into life," "perfect," "saved," and "kingdom of God." Each of these terms refer to salvation.

**Matthew 19:13 - 30** Then little children were brought to Him that He might put His hands on them and pray, but the disciples rebuked them. [14]But Jesus said, "Let the little children come to Me, and do not forbid them; for of such is the kingdom of heaven." [15]And He laid His hands on them and departed from there. [16]Now behold, one came and said to Him, "Good Teacher, what good thing shall I do that I may have eternal life?" [17]So He said to him, "Why do you call Me good? No one is good but One, that is, God. But if you want to enter into life, keep the commandments." [18]He said to Him, "Which ones?" Jesus said, "'You shall not murder,' 'You shall not commit adultery,' 'You shall not steal,' 'You shall not bear false witness,' [19]'Honor your father and your mother,' and, 'You shall love your neighbor as yourself.'" [20]The young man said to Him, "All these things I have kept from my youth. What do I still lack?" [21]Jesus said to him, "If you want to be perfect, go, sell what you have and give to the poor, and you will have treasure in heaven; and come, follow Me." [22]But when the young man heard that saying, he went away sorrowful, for he had great possessions. [23]Then Jesus said to His disciples, "Assuredly, I say to you that it is hard for a rich man to enter the kingdom of heaven. [24]And again I say to you, it is easier for a camel to go through the eye of a needle than for a rich man to enter the kingdom of God." [25]When His disciples heard it, they were greatly astonished, saying, "Who then can be saved?" [26]But Jesus looked at them and said to them, "With men this is impossible, but with God all things are possible." [27]Then Peter answered and said to Him, "See, we have left all and followed You. Therefore what shall we have?" [28]So Jesus said to them, "Assuredly I say to you, that in the regeneration, when the Son of Man sits on the throne of His glory, you who have followed Me will also sit on twelve thrones, judging the twelve tribes of Israel. [29]And everyone who has left houses or brothers or sisters or father or mother or wife or children or lands, for My name's sake, shall receive a hundredfold, and inherit eternal life. [30]But many who are first will be last, and the last first." [NKJ]

Based on what you have highlighted about salvation, how can one be saved?

*Jesus didn't say that a rich man could not enter the kingdom of heaven. He just said that it was extremely difficult. He indicated that extreme difficulty with an extreme illustration!*

Look at Matthew 19:23-24. What's harder and what's easier and what's the point?

> Despite sermonic lore based on medieval tradition and modern anecdotes, there is no early historical evidence for the existence of a small gate in Jerusalem, supposedly called the Needle's Eye, through which a camel on its knees could barely squeeze. This mistaken understanding weakens Jesus' hyperbole and implies that it is not actually impossible for rich people to enter the kingdom.[111]

*The disciples "were totally amazed" at Jesus statement. The common Jewish perspective was that riches were a sign of God's blessing. This was based on Scriptures such as Deuteronomy 28:1-14. So they were confused – if the rich were blessed, wouldn't it be easier for them to be saved than other men and women? So they asked, "**Who** then can be saved?"*

*The discussion shifts now from being about a rich man's salvation to being about any man's salvation.*

We need to look at Jesus' response one phrase at a time:

**Matthew 19:26:** "With _____, _____ is _____."
What does "this" refer to?

What is "impossible"?

Please look up the definition for the following word:
**Impossible: Strong's #102**
**Greek word:**
**Greek definition:**

Do you agree that, humanly speaking, it is impossible for anyone to be saved? What reason is there for any man or woman to receive salvation? What can anyone do to be saved?

The second half of Jesus' response is:

**Matthew 19:26:** "but with _____, all things are _____."

*But God. Only God. He is able – to save to the uttermost. He can do for us what we cannot do for ourselves. That's why it's called being saved! He rescues...out of slavery to sin, out of despair, out of death.*

According to the following verses, how does God save?

**Matthew 1:21**

**Acts 16:30-31**

**1 Corinthians 1:18**

**Ephesians 2:8-9**

**Titus 3:5**

**Hebrews 7:25**

**1 Peter 1:3-5**

*Hallelujah! Praise the Lord! I've been saved! What about you?*

Has God done the impossible in your life? If so, how did He do it? If not, ask Him to do it right now!!

*Now what? The comments in Matthew 19:13-30 set our minds on eternity. And Peter, probably speaking for all the disciples, wants to know what the future holds. Commentators say that he and the disciples were giving themselves a pat on the back for already forsaking all and following Jesus. So what would they get? The rich young ruler had been promised treasure in heaven. What would the disciples' reward be?*

*What a wise, patient, gracious Teacher Jesus is. He answers their question.*

In Matthew 19:28, what does Jesus promise specifically to His twelve disciples?

The concept of "the regeneration" would not be a bit ambiguous to the average Israelite. It was the belief of the Jews that the Messiah, after His advent, would create a new heaven and a new earth. [112]

What will happen according to Isaiah 66:22?

And Hosea 3:4-5?

And Ezekiel 37:24-25?

And Daniel 7:13-14?

In Matthew 19:29, how is following Jesus as a disciple described? What promise is made to everyone who makes this commitment?

*The reward to the twelve disciples and the rewards to all disciples exceed the sacrifice required!*

# Unit Nine    Matthew 20:1 — 23:36

# JESUS PREDICTS THE FUTURE

*The lesson in rewards isn't over yet. The chapter division at the end of verse 30 doesn't make much sense. The parable in the next passage is definitely related to Peter's question that we considered previously.*

*But please don't consider it a slight to Jesus' teaching through the next parable when we move quickly through it. Jesus is about to go up to Jerusalem (Matthew 20:17) , and we need to keep moving with Him.*

Ask the Holy Spirit to lead you to
focus on the Word of God today.

Please fill in the chart below based on Matthew 20:1-16.

| Description of Laborers | Hour Hired | Agreed upon Wages | Type of labor | Wages Paid | Reaction when Paid |
|---|---|---|---|---|---|
| | | | | | |
| | | | | | |
| | | | | | |

**Matthew 19:30** "But many who are first will be last, and the last first."

**Matthew 20:16** "So the last will be first, and the first last. For many are called, but few chosen."

*Matthew 19:30 and Matthew 20:16 form an "inclusio" – which is a literary device, like the two pieces of bread in a sandwich! They hold the meat in the middle. Because 19:30 is clearly part of Jesus' response to Peter, that means that this parable should be read in conjunction with the previous passage. We need to remember the rich young ruler and the poor ole' disciples. Both were promised rewards for following Jesus.*

What is the perspective of the landowner in Matthew 20:13-15?

*One more final comment about the inclusion verses. What do they mean anyway? There is no context to make us think that the Jews are the first and the Gentiles are the last. But the context does present the rich young ruler and the disciples. "The last shall be first" (Matthew 19:30) is a **promise** to the disciples because they will gain great reward in heaven. "The first shall be last" (Matthew 20:16) is a **warning** to the disciples not to assume that reward is an automatic entitlement to them.*[113]

*Jesus and the disciples have been talking about the future, about eternal life, and about rewards. But Jesus' future first includes suffering, and that time is drawing near. He has been preparing His disciples both implicitly and explicitly.*

Note the implied references to His suffering, death, and resurrection in the following verses:

**Matthew 10:21**

**Matthew 10:28**

**Matthew 10:38**

**Matthew 12:14**

**Matthew 16:4**

**Matthew 17:12**

*Unless we are absolutely forced to talk about it, death is usually a subject that we would rather not discuss. Especially the death of someone close to us. It's easier to say, "let's not talk about that." It was time for Jesus to talk about it and to talk more directly than He had done before. He only shares this with His twelve disciples.*

Look at the predictions that Jesus made regarding His death and resurrection. Highlight the parallels in one color and the differences in another color.

**Matthew 16:21** From that time Jesus Christ began to show His disciples that He must go to Jerusalem, and suffer many things from the elders and chief priests and scribes, and be killed, and be raised up on the third day. NAS

**Matthew 17:22** And while they were gathering together in Galilee, Jesus said to them, "The Son of Man is going to be delivered into the hands of men; 23 and they will kill Him, and He will be raised on the third day." And they were deeply grieved. NAS

**Matthew 20:17-19** And as Jesus was about to go up to Jerusalem, He took the twelve *disciples* aside by themselves, and on the way He said to them, 18 "Behold, we are going up to Jerusalem; and the Son of Man will be delivered to the chief priests and scribes, and they will condemn Him to death, 19 and will deliver Him to the Gentiles to mock and scourge and crucify *Him*, and on the third day He will be raised up." NAS

What two critical points did Jesus repeat in every statement in the previous verses?


What did Jesus predict in Matthew 20:18-19 that had not been mentioned explicitly prior to this time?


*This is an ominous and dramatic statement. The time has almost come. They are on their way to Jerusalem even as Jesus is speaking. Given the grief expressed after the second prediction, and the silence of the disciples after the third, we can imagine their shock at the horrific description of what was to come.*

*It seems that Jesus' suffering was too hard for the disciples to talk about. They'd rather move on, to talk again about those rewards they would receive. The sons of Zebedee (James and John) had a special request.*

**Please read Matthew 20:20-28.**

Who initiates the conversation and why? (verses 20-21)


Who does Jesus answer and what does He say? (verses 22-23)


The "cup" throughout Scripture refers figuratively to one's divinely appointed destiny, whether it was one of blessing and salvation (Ps. 16:5;116:13) or of wrath and disaster (Isa. 51:17; Jer. 25:15-29). Jesus is referring to His forthcoming cup of suffering on the cross, to which He has just given His third prediction. [114]

What do you learn about Jesus' relationship with His Father based on His response?


*Have you noticed a theme since Matthew 18:1? What has been concerning the disciples? "Who is the greatest?" "What do we get?" "Can you save us the good seats?" The desire for recognition in Matthew 20:20-21 is in stark contrast to Jesus' dedication to suffering in Matthew 20:17-19. Jesus didn't mince words as He pointed out to James and John that "to be identified with Jesus' future glory means first to be identified with His suffering and death." [115]*

What did the other disciples think about this discussion? Was their attitude much different from the two brothers'? (verse 24)

*This discussion between the disciples and Jesus opened the door for a critical lesson and a crucial declaration. Jesus will teach the disciples that true greatness is seen in servanthood which will lead Him to proclaim, for the first time, the reason for His coming suffering.*

What was Jesus' "upside-down" exhortation to the disciples? (verses 25-27)

What did Jesus clearly say about His death? (verse 28)

> Ransom: *lutron*: 1) the price for redeeming, ransom. 1a) paid for slaves, captives; 1b) for the ransom of life; 2) to liberate many from misery and the penalty of their sins. [116]

What was the impact of Jesus giving His life as a ransom, based on the following verses?

**2 Corinthians 5:15**

**Galatians 1:3-4**

**Ephesians 5:25-27**

**Hebrews 9:12-14**

*His death and resurrection make the difference in our lives. It wasn't until after Jesus' death, resurrection, and sending of the Holy Spirit that the disciples were able to really understand what He had been teaching them. When you are ransomed out of sin and self-centeredness, you aren't a slave to them anymore. That's when you are free to be a slave – a servant – to others.*

Does Jesus' teaching in Matthew 20:25-27 makes sense to you? Do you live like it does?

How does the event in Matthew 20:29-34 demonstrate the lesson He just taught? Notice attitude of the crowd and Jesus' attitude and action.

*Not only does that short account of the miracle demonstrate the servanthood of Jesus, it also highlights His identity as the Messiah once again. The two men might have been blind, but they could see that Jesus was the Son of David, the promised Messiah, of whom it was prophesied that He would give sight to the blind. Remember, no one but Jesus **ever** did that before! It was a big deal! "And immediately their eyes received sight, and they followed Him." Right into the city of Jerusalem. It's time. Jesus has one week left.*

# JESUS ARRIVES IN JERUSALEM

*I had the opportunity to ride a donkey down a mountain a few years ago. I passed on that adventure.. They smelled. It didn't look like it would be too fun, slowly clip-clopping on the back of that tired looking animal. I've ridden a horse down a hill though, probably my best horse ride ever! I was 16 and almost fearless and free. Horses are strong, stately, and far superior to donkeys.*

*Jesus just asked for a donkey to ride down the Mount of Olives. He was still modeling humility. We call this next passage the Triumphal Entry because of the crowds waving palm branches and shouting "Hosanna!" Jesus actions really classify it as a Humble Entry instead.*

> Please pray that the Holy Spirit will give you a
> desire to know Jesus more intimately.

**Please read Matthew 21:1-11.**

What's your favorite part of Jesus' entrance into Jerusalem?

*Just wondering...do you think the two disciples Jesus sent to get the donkey and colt were James and John? Maybe giving them a little practice in serving? We don't know. It doesn't matter. I just noticed that He sent two disciples.*

What does the quote from Zechariah 9:9 (Matthew 21:5) emphasize about the identity of Jesus?

What does the quote from Psalm 118:26 (Matthew 21:9) tell you about Jesus?

Look up the definition for the following word:
**Hosanna: Strong's #5614**
**Greek word:**
**Greek definition:**

*Hosanna is actually a Hebrew word, isn't it? The people were crying out a refrain of praise and prayer. They didn't really mean it though; they were just caught up in the moment.*

Based on Matthew 21:9-11, did the crowd or the people of Jerusalem know who Jesus was? What did they think?

After arriving in the city, where did Jesus go and what did He do? Read Matthew 21:12-16 and summarize what you learn.

How did these actions demonstrate Jesus' identity as the Messiah, the Son of God, the Son of David? What did Jesus say Himself that indicated it?

How did the chief priests and scribes feel about all this?

*"Then He left them and went out of the city to Bethany, and He lodged there." (Matthew 21:17) It wasn't time for a confrontation with them yet.*

How did the next day begin? Read Matthew 21:18-19 and note your answer.

*Jesus didn't explain why He cursed the fig tree and the disciples didn't ask Him. Commentators, however, have explained that: "the cursing of the fruitless fig tree portrays the fruitless religious leaders, whose temple was just cleared." [117] The dried up tree symbolized judgment on the leaders and the coming destruction of the temple which would occur in 70 AD.*

Review what has been a common theme in Matthew and summarize Matthew 3:10; 7:17-20; and 12:33.

The disciples didn't ask why; they asked…how? What did Jesus tell the disciples in this teachable moment? (verses 20-22)

*Do you remember this illustration of faith? In Matthew 17:20, He told them, "It was because of your little faith. I tell you the truth, if you have faith the size of a mustard seed, you will say to this mountain, 'Move from here to there,' and it will move; nothing will be impossible for you."*

*Does the word "impossible" bring anything particular to mind? It won't be long before the disciples have the opportunity to reflect on Jesus' teachings; and through the enlightenment of the Holy Spirit, they'll put it all together. As they exercise their faith, and pray according to God's will, and testify to the salvation provided through Jesus' sacrifice, they will see mountains of misery cast into the sea. Men and women, old and young, rich and poor, slave and free, first and last – can be saved. With man, this is impossible, but with God all things are possible.*

What does Micah 7:18-19 say?

*The religious leaders of the day were fruitless, just like the fig tree. The disciples would be faithful and like a tree full of figs.*

What's on your branches? Just leaves or lots of fruit?

*It always gets back to that same question, doesn't it? Are you living out your faith as a devoted disciple? Jesus was **radical.** Are you?*

---

Lesson Three: Matthew 21:23-45

## JESUS TEACHES AT THE TEMPLE

*The Monday morning headline in **The Temple Times** read: "Prophet Destroying Profits in the Court." The article which followed noted that the renowned prophet Jesus of Nazareth had returned to Jerusalem and was wreaking havoc among the businessmen in the Temple Court. Not only did He toss tables to the ground and scatter valuables throughout the Temple grounds, He also reveled in the adoration of children swarming around Him. On the other hand, His presence was not completely undesirable because He knew how to make the blind regain their vision and He administered physical therapy to those who could not walk. The ruling Chief Priest, when interviewed, said, 'We'll be asking Jesus a few questions tomorrow about His activities.'"*

Please take time today to prepare your heart
to hear the teachings of Jesus.

**Please read Matthew 21:23-27.**

What do the chief priests and elders say is concerning them?

*Did they really not know? If they had been asked "by what authority does Jesus say that He heals the sick?" wouldn't they have said: "He indicates that it is from God"? They just wanted to make Him say it outright, so that they could later accuse Him.*

What did they say when reasoning among themselves that indicated the real assessment of their hearts?

*Jesus wouldn't tell them what they wanted to hear. Instead He tells them what they don't want to hear. The next two parables are just for the chief priests and Pharisees.*

Please note from Matthew 21:45, their reaction after hearing them; then we'll go back and see what the parables say.

Please read the Parable of the Two Sons: **Matthew 21:28-32.**

Did the chief priests have any trouble answering Jesus' question at this point?

What parallels does Jesus draw between the parable and real life that would have shocked the religious leaders?

First son –

Second son –

The will of the father –

---

> The religious leaders are like the son who agreed but did nothing. They were externally obedient to the law, but when God sent His messenger, John the Baptist, they did not obey God's message through him. [118]

---

Look back at Matthew 21:23-27. Then read Matthew 21:32. Why was it so important for the religious leaders to believe what John the Baptist preached? (Need a reminder? Matthew 3:11-17; 11:10.)

*The religious leaders were in double jeopardy. This interaction shows that 1) they didn't believe John or Jesus, and 2) their works didn't match their words.*

By what authority do you believe Jesus did all of His works?


Does your walk match your talk?


*The chief priests and elders haven't left the Temple yet. They are still standing with Jesus. He has another parable for them.*

Please read the Parable of the Wicked Vinedressers in Matthew 21:33-45. "Fruit" is a key word to watch for in this passage.

What did the landowner want from the vinedressers?

What was the shocking behavior of the vinedressers?

What did the religious leaders think should be done by the landowner?


*How did the chief priests and Pharisees perceive that this parable was about them? They knew that the Scriptures referred to Israel as the vineyard of the Lord (Isaiah 5:7), and they knew that they were against the One who called Himself the Son of Man – another messianic title for the Son of God.*

Jesus helped them understand it too. What did He tell them in verses 42-43?

A common view is that the kingdom is taken away from the Jewish people as a whole and given to the predominantly Gentile church. But a preferable view is that the kingdom is to be taken away from the disobedient religious leaders and given to the twelve disciples who will lead Jesus' church. [119]

*The twelve disciples may have become the new vinedressers but they didn't keep the work of the vineyard all to themselves. Peter eloquently refers to this parable in his exhortation to believers.*

What does 1 Peter 2:7-9 tell you?


*While the Parable of the Wicked Vinedressers is a condemnation of the religious leaders, it is also a prediction of Jesus' suffering. The foreboding tone is increasing.*

What do the chief priests and Pharisees want to do, according to Matthew 21:46?


*Wait. That's what they had to do.*

Lesson Four: Matthew 22:1-14

# JESUS CHOOSES WEDDING GUESTS

*Still standing at the Temple, the chief priests and Pharisees listen to another parable about themselves. "The kingdom of heaven is like..." The opening of the next parable sets the stage for it being not only about the unbelieving religious leaders but also about the nation of Israel and all others as well.*

Ask the Spirit to help you understand today's lesson
and that you have been chosen by God .

**Please read Matthew 22:1-14.**

There are a few similarities to the parable in Matthew 21:33-41. Who is represented by the landowner and king?

Who do the servants represent?

In Matthew 22:3-6, those first invited to the wedding represent Israel. Given the context of the previous parable, who specifically was "not willing to come"? What did they do to the servants?

*What??? An invitation to the royal wedding feast, at the king's house, and they **kill** the messengers? Parables tell a normal story with surprising twists. John the Baptist was dead. Jesus soon would be. Disciples would be martyred too. This is a parable with the big picture in mind.*

What was the king's response to the violence of the invited guests?

*Prophecy in the parables – Jesus' death and Jerusalem's destruction. The warning signs were being given. We know they were ignored.*

The wedding feast will still take place. Who is invited since the first guests refused to come?

*"They gathered together all whom they found, both bad and good." Previous parables of the kingdom of heaven taught us that there will be both bad and good until the end of the age when the angels separate the wicked from the righteous. This is truly one of the mysteries of the kingdom of heaven. Not everyone who says that they belong to Jesus does.*

*One guest stands out in the crowd. His clothes are all wrong.*

What treatment does the improperly attired man receive?

---

> Jesus warns that the disciples' troubles will not come merely from outsiders. They cannot become complacent and forget the necessity of obedience to all that Jesus has commanded. Soon Jesus' betrayal will make this point crystal clear: Judas Iscariot [called "friend" Matt. 26:50] was called but not chosen. [120]

*Believe Jesus. Follow Him. Walk by faith. Do good works.*

According to the following verses, what are disciples supposed to wear, no matter what the latest style is?

**Psalm 30:11**

**1 Timothy 2:9-10**

**1 Peter 5:5**

**Revelation 19:8**

Let's get dressed up – we've got a wedding party to attend! What would you add as accessories to finish your outfit?

What does Matthew 22:14 say?

*We won't ignore the elephant in the room. It's okay. He won't hurt anyone. He's one of our sovereign God's creations, just as sweet little loving puppies and beautiful graceful peacocks are. I'm talking about the elephant called "election."*

Please look up the following words and definitions:
**Called: Strong's #2822 (and root word #2564)**
**Greek word:**
**Greek definition:**

**Chosen: Strong's #1588 (and root word #1586)**
**Greek word:**
**Greek definition:**

Note what you learn about those who are called from the verses below.

**Romans 1:5-6**

**Romans 8:28-30**

**1 Corinthians 1:9**

**2 Timothy 1:9**

**Hebrews 9:15**

**1 Peter 5:10**

Note what you learn about those who are chosen from the verses below.

**1 Chronicles 16:13**

**Isaiah 42:1**

**John 15:16**

**Ephesians 1:4**

**Colossians 3:12**

**1 Peter 1:1-2**

**James 2:5**

*To be called is to be invited. And an invitation includes an "R.S.V.P." A response is required. "Many are called." (Matthew 22:14)*

---

"Many" without the article is a common Semitic [Jewish] universalizing expression, which is normally translated "everyone" or "all." By the expression "many are invited," Jesus points to a universal invitation to the kingdom of heaven. [121]

---

Please read Matthew 22:1-14, considering the invitation given to many. Why didn't everyone who was invited come to the wedding?

---

While there is an open invitation to the kingdom, from the divine perspective it is only God's sovereign choice that effects salvation. From a human perspective it is only those who respond to the call appropriately that are part of the banquet. Only an appropriate response reveals God's divine election. [122]

---

*This is a mystery in salvation. God invites everyone. Everyone has an opportunity to respond to Him. God chooses some. Everyone who is chosen responds to the invitation.*

*I know. That's a really big elephant in the room. You probably feel like he's going to crush someone. But he belongs to God. Even if you can't get your arms around him or if you don't want to go near him, I encourage you to respect him. Just let him stand there and be in awe of the wisdom and ways of His creator. That elephant leads you to the Lamb. The only thing he crushes is a snake.*

How does Revelation 17:14 sum it all up?

Write out a prayer of praise to God for His invitation to enter the kingdom of heaven.

Lesson Five: Matthew 22:15-46

## JESUS AMAZES HIS OPPONENTS

*He knew what was coming. With determination to do God's will, Jesus continued discussions with all those who were mounting an attack against Him. They were also determined – to destroy Him one way or another.*

Please pray for a hunger to know the Word of God
and to rightly apply it to your life.

Read through the four interactions on the next page. Use three colors for highlighting or marking: one for those who challenged Jesus, one for the way they address Jesus, and one for the Scriptures quoted. (You may need to look at your own Bible to determine quotations.)

**Matthew 22:15-46**   Then the Pharisees went and counseled together how they might trap Him in what He said. [16] And they sent their disciples to Him, along with the Herodians, saying, "Teacher, we know that You are truthful and teach the way of God in truth, and defer to no one; for You are not partial to any. [17] Tell us therefore, what do You think? Is it lawful to give a poll-tax to Caesar, or not?" [18] But Jesus perceived their malice, and said, "Why are you testing Me, you hypocrites? [19] Show Me the coin used for the poll-tax." And they brought Him a denarius. [20] And He said to them, "Whose likeness and inscription is this?" [21] They said to Him, "Caesar's." Then He said to them, "Then render to Caesar the things that are Caesar's; and to God the things that are God's." [22] And hearing this, they marveled, and leaving Him, they went away.

[23] On that day some Sadducees (who say there is no resurrection) came to Him and questioned Him, [24] saying, "Teacher, Moses said, 'If a man dies, having no children, his brother as next of kin shall marry his wife, and raise up an offspring to his brother.' [25] "Now there were seven brothers with us; and the first married and died, and having no offspring left his wife to his brother; [26] so also the second, and the third, down to the seventh. [27] And last of all, the woman died. [28] In the resurrection therefore whose wife of the seven shall she be? For they all had her." [29] But Jesus answered and said to them, "You are mistaken, not understanding the Scriptures, or the power of God. [30] For in the resurrection they neither marry, nor are given in marriage, but are like angels in heaven. [31] But regarding the resurrection of the dead, have you not read that which was spoken to you by God, saying, [32] 'I am the God of Abraham, and the God of Isaac, and the God of Jacob '? He is not the God of the dead but of the living." [33] And when the multitudes heard this, they were astonished at His teaching.

[34] But when the Pharisees heard that He had put the Sadducees to silence, they gathered themselves together. [35] And one of them, a lawyer, asked Him a question, testing Him, [36] "Teacher, which is the great commandment in the Law?" [37] And He said to him, "'You shall love the LORD your God with all your heart, and with all your soul, and with all your mind.' [38] This is the great and foremost commandment. [39] The second is like it, 'You shall love your neighbor as yourself.' [40] On these two commandments depend the whole Law and the Prophets."

[41] Now while the Pharisees were gathered together, Jesus asked them a question, [42] saying, "What do you think about the Christ, whose son is He?" They said to Him, "The son of David." [43] He said to them, "Then how does David in the Spirit call Him 'Lord,' saying, [44] 'The Lord said to my LORD, "Sit at My right hand, Until I put Thine enemies beneath Thy feet"? [45] If David then calls Him 'Lord,' how is He his son?" [46] And no one was able to answer Him a word, nor did anyone dare from that day on to ask Him another question. [NAS]

*They were still at the Temple. Jerusalem's brightest and boldest attempted to trap Jesus in His teachings so that they could accuse Him and silence Him.*

What groups approached Jesus?

1.

2.

3.

4.

What questions did they ask Him?

1.

2.

3.

*Jesus' concise answers were:*

1. *Render to Caesar the things that are Caesar's; and to God the things that are God's.*

2. *In the resurrection they neither marry nor are given in marriage, but are like angels in heaven. God is not the God of the dead but of the living*

3. *You shall love the Lord your God with all your heart, and with all your soul, and with all your mind. You shall love your neighbor as yourself. On these two commandments depend the whole Law and the Prophets.*

*Give to God what belongs to Him. He is the God of the living. Love Him and love others. You can't dispute any of those teachings.*

What were the responses to Jesus' statements?

1.

2.

3.

What is your response to Jesus' first statement? How do you give to God what belongs to Him?

*What is your response to the statement to the Sadducees? We need to dig into that one a little more. Matthew told us that the Sadducees didn't believe in the resurrection. That's why "they are so sad... you see...."! (Just had to quote that children's song.) "They think of resurrection and the afterlife as mere reanimation to life as before."* [123] *Guess what – they didn't believe in angels either!*

*Jesus proves the truth of resurrection by quoting Exodus 3:6. The resurrection is going to bring about the final transformation of believers. It will bring about the final moments of sanctification which will lead to glorification which is a new and improved state of being. Men and women with glorified bodies will be like the angels. Pay attention to that word "like"! It means "similar to," not "identical to."*

What do you learn from 1 Corinthians 15:42-44?

And from 1 Corinthians 15:51-54?

Now, what's your response to the truth of the resurrection?

Then and now, the greatest commandments are to be our way of life. What is your response to that? Are they?

For a reminder of what that will look like, turn to and note the description of love in 1 Corinthians 13:4-7.

*After answering each of His challengers' questions, it was Jesus' turn to ask one. He gets right to the point! "What do you think about the Christ, whose son is He?" They didn't have any trouble with the answer to that one: "The son of David." The son of David is a man: a human. They could grasp that.*

*It was the next two questions that baffled them.*

What was Jesus' question in Matthew 22:43?

What was Jesus' question in Matthew 22:45?

*If the Messiah is a descendant of great King David, how can David call him Lord? That was Jesus' first question. How can David give him greater authority and honor than he himself had? The father is to receive honor from his sons, not vise versa.*

*If the Messiah is Lord, then how is he a son, a descendant of David? Matthew has demonstrated repeatedly that Jesus is the Son of God. How is the Son of God the son of David? The Pharisees didn't know. We can't explain the answer either, except to say that "with God nothing is impossible." This is the mind-boggling truth that Jesus is God and man. Amazing.*

On this extremely sad note ends Matthew's story of Jesus' conflict with the religious leaders in Jerusalem. Nothing more can be said, and unfortunately, the conflict remains a theological watershed today as Judaism expects a human Messiah and Christianity worships a divine one. [124]

What is your response to the truth that Jesus is God and man?

Lesson Six: Matthew 23:1-36

# JESUS FINDS FAULT WITH THE PHARISEES AND THEIR FRIENDS

*What a day to be at the Temple! If you were interested at all in that man named Jesus, you would have wanted to hear what He had to say to the religious leaders. Apparently many gathered around Him as the scribes, Herodians, Sadducees, and Pharisees interrogated Him hoping that He would incriminate Himself.*

*The guilt was on their own heads instead. They became the examples of what not to do. Jesus delivers His last public message.*

Ask the Spirit to teach you today
through the words of Jesus.

**Please read Matthew 23:1-12.**

To whom does Jesus speak?

*His first few words probably sounded pretty good to the Pharisees still standing around Jesus. Nodding their heads soberly, they may have thought, "That's right. Listen to us. We teach the commands of Moses." Then the nodding stopped. "What did He just say?"*

What did Jesus tell the crowd to do and not to do?

After reading the following commentaries, in the chart below, match the faults of the Pharisees with the corresponding phrases.

**They bind heavy burdens...** - This phrase is derived from the custom of loading animals. The load or burden is bound up and then laid on the beast. So the Pharisees appointed weighty burdens, or grievous and heavy precepts, and insisted that the people should obey them, though they lent no assistance.... The Pharisees were rigid in requiring that all the people should pay the taxes, give of their property, comply with every part of the law with the utmost rigor, yet they indulged themselves, and bore as little of the expense and trouble as possible; so that, where they could avoid it, they would not lend the least aid to the people in the toils and expense of their religious rites. [125]

**The phylactery** was a leather box, cube-shaped, closed with an attached flap and bound to the person by a leather band. There were two kinds: (1) one to be bound to the inner side of the left arm, and near the elbow, so that with the bending of the arm it would rest over the heart... and the end of the string, or band, finally wound around the middle finger of the hand, "a sign upon thy hand" (Deut. 6:8). This box had one compartment containing one or all of the four passages: Exodus 13:9; 13:16; Deuteronomy 6:8; 11:18. (2) Another was to be bound in the center of the forehead, "between thine eyes" (Deut. 6:8). [126]

**The rabbi** was generally a master of the Torah, and the title usually refers to the head of a rabbinical school. The association with these schools tended to set them aside somewhat from the populace. The school was a holy community, and the people regarded the members as a whole with great deference. [127]

**The use of the term "father"** as a title of honor, respect, and authority had deep roots in ancient Judaism. "Father" occurs regularly in rabbinic sources as a title for esteemed scholars and rabbis. Jesus warns against elevating religious leaders to a place where they usurp the authority due to God alone. [128]

**The term "leader"** [Teacher, Master] occurs in Greek literature to designate especially a private tutor, which may point to the individual authority an instructor has over a student. Jesus' disciples are not to seek out personal authority as "master" over other disciples, because as the Messiah, Jesus alone is Master. [129]

Consider the following faults of the Pharisees. Which phrases above correspond to them? (The chart on the next page will help you!)

**Hypocrisy -**

**Legalism -**

**Pride -**

**Power Hungry -**

**Usurping God's Authority -**

| Faults | Matthew 23:2-10 |
|---|---|
| Hypocrisy | [2] The scribes and the Pharisees have seated themselves in the chair of Moses; [3] therefore all that they tell you, do and observe, but do not do according to their deeds; for they say things, and do not do them. |
| Legalism | [4] And they tie up heavy loads, and lay them on men's shoulders; but they themselves are unwilling to move them with so much as a finger. |
| Pride | [5] But they do all their deeds to be noticed by men; for they broaden their phylacteries, and lengthen the tassels of their garments. |
| Power hungry | [6] And they love the place of honor at banquets, and the chief seats in the synagogues, [7] and respectful greetings in the market places, and being called by men, Rabbi. |
| Usurping God's authority | [8] But do not be called Rabbi; for One is your Teacher, and you are all brothers. [9] And do not call anyone on earth your father; for One is your Father, He who is in heaven. [10] And do not be called leaders; for One is your Leader, that is, Christ. NAS |

Do you ever become pharisaical? Which, if any, of these faults do you sometimes find in your own life?

*Jesus never leaves you all tied up. Unlike the Pharisees, He exhorts and encourages. He highlights the problem and helps the person. He is the perfect religious leader, the true High Priest, who sympathizes with our weaknesses, who has lived up to the letter and the love of the law. Remember, He had just declared the greatest and second greatest commandments of all (Matthew 22:37-40). Every word of God was based on those decrees.*

How do the Pharisees' faults break the two greatest commandments?

At the end of His message to the crowd and disciples, what did Jesus tell them to do and not do?

How does this encouragement correspond to the two greatest commandments?

*Jesus' humility and servanthood was seen by what He did and did not do. His attitude was demonstrated with action.*

Do you need a new attitude – of humility and servanthood? What do you need to do or not do in order to demonstrate that attitude with action?

*Jesus was invading the religious leaders' territory and tearing down their traditions. Tradition! They wanted to keep things the way they were. This "new kid on the block" had to go.*

*The scribes and Pharisees must have been in shock at what they had just heard from Jesus. Shock and awe were about to multiply! Jesus had more to say to them.*

**Please read Matthew 23:13-36.**

What does Jesus repeatedly declare to the scribes and Pharisees? It's just three little words, but they are disastrous.

*I've looked up the definition for the following word for you.*

> **Woe: Strong's #3759**
> **Greek word:** οὐαί   *(pronounced: oo-ah'ee), particle of interjection*
> **Greek definition:** A primary exclamation of grief; (1) expressing extreme displeasure and calling for retributive pain on someone or something *woe! alas!* (Mt 11:2); doubled or tripled for emphasis (Rev 8:1; 18:1); (2) *woe, disaster, calamity* (Rev 9:1) [130]

What does this definition tell you about Jesus' perspective toward the religious leaders?

Jesus tells it like it is. What does He call the scribes and Pharisees in the groups of verses below?

**Matthew 23:13, 14, 15, 23, 25, 27, 29 –**

**Matthew 23:16, 17, 19, 24, 26 –**

**Matthew 23:33 –**

Why does Jesus call them hypocrites?

Why does Jesus call them blind?

*The scribes were the scholars of the Scriptures, zealous defenders of the Law, and the teachers of the people. The Pharisees also studied the Scriptures and concerned themselves with the oral interpretations of the Law. Both of these groups were intimately acquainted with the Word of God and its truths. Those who have the Scriptures are accountable for how they respond to them.*

*We who study the Bible, as we are now doing, are accountable as well. We could consider our own lives in light of each of the woes against the scribes and Pharisees. But let's take a broader examination of ourselves.*

You who have the Word of God in your hands…are you a hypocrite, a pretender in any way? Does your lifestyle match your belief?

You who have the Word of God in your hands…are you blind or foolish? Are you denying or ignoring particular truths in Scripture, as if they are not applicable to you?

*Matthew 23 is Jesus' prophetic pronouncement against the religious leaders of His lifetime. They carried on the tradition of rejecting true servants and prophets of God just as those before them had done. Jesus prophesies publicly with grief as well as anger and alarm that excruciating consequences will come to them. They are condemned as sons of hell.*

*One commentator said that Jesus' prophecy against the leaders lacks any word of grace. But I propose to you that the warning itself is a word of grace and an opportunity to turn from their rejection of truth and to turn to their Redeemer. As long as a warning exists, there is still time to change.*

The Scriptures in Matthew have warned you repeatedly of eternal consequences if you aren't following Jesus. Have you made the necessary changes?

# Unit Ten    Matthew 24:1 — 26:75

Lesson 1  Jesus tells of tribulations

Lesson 2  Jesus announces an abomination

Lesson 3  Jesus prepares with parables

Lesson 4  Jesus' concluding remarks

Lesson 5  Jesus' last days

Lesson 6  Jesus surrenders his will

# JESUS TELLS OF TRIBULATIONS

*The end is near. I don't say that with a smile. We have watched as Jesus has journeyed step by step through the land of Israel preaching His message: "Repent, for the kingdom of heaven is at hand." His final messages were preached in Jerusalem, in the courts of the temple, the house of the Lord.*

> Pray that you will believe that all Scripture is useful for teaching and training in righteousness.

**According to Matthew 23:37-39:**

How does Jesus express His compassion for the city?

How does Jesus express the clash of His will with that of the city?

What will happen to the house of the Lord?

What is the bittersweet promise?

> Jesus' compassion is palpable. Other touching biblical laments pale in comparison with this one. Jesus is deeply moved for His people and for His city despite the ongoing opposition of its leaders and the horrible sufferings that are still ahead. Christians today must ponder Jesus' compassion for His people and reflect on their own level of concern for Jews. An arrogant attitude toward non-Christians is always inappropriate, but it is especially despicable when it concerns the Jewish people. [131]

How do you feel and how do you act toward Jewish people today?

*Jesus makes more comments that prompt questions from the disciples. They are still trying to sort things out. What is going on? What's going to happen? When is it going to happen?*

**Please read Matthew 24:1-3.**

Where is Jesus when the disciples come to Him?

What are their specific questions?

*This is the introduction to the fifth and final sermon that Jesus gives. Matthew 24 and 25 contain the sermon called the Mount Olivet Discourse. Now you know why!*

*Buckle your seat belts. There's a lot of turbulence ahead.*

You shouldn't be surprised at your first assignment. I want you to see the sermon in its entirety. This will be the main part of your lesson. **Please read Matthew 24 and 25.** (You don't have to understand everything you read!)

Now, please briefly describe the topic covered in each of the following passages of the sermon. Keep it simple.

**Matthew 24:4-14**


**Matthew 24:15-28**


**Matthew 24:29-36**


**Matthew 24:37-44**


**Matthew 24:45-51**


**Matthew 25:1-13**


**Matthew 25:14-30**


**Matthew 25:31-46**


*There are many specific details mentioned in this prophetic sermon. But there are also several general lessons to be learned. Alertness, trustworthiness, fruitfulness, service and compassion are to characterize followers of Jesus, especially in the end-times. We'll consider these after we contemplate the events described.*

*The first three passages above are Jesus' response to the disciples' question: "what will be the sign of Your coming and of the end of the age?" There is no mention of rapture in these verses. The disciples were expecting Jesus to come and rule as King, so now they were asking when He would return (after His death) and reign. Jesus describes what will happen before He returns to earth as King of Kings to reign over His kingdom.*

*Warren Wiersbe points out the parallels between Jesus' prophecy in Matthew 24 and John's prophecy in Revelation 6.*

Note what the verses say in the chart below.

| Matthew 24 | Events | Revelation 6 |
|---|---|---|
| v.4-5 | **False Christs** | v.1-2 |
| v.6 | **Wars** | v.3-4 |
| v.7a | **Famines** | v.5-6 |
| v.7b-8 | **Death** | v.7-8 |
| v.9 | **Martyrs** | v.9-11 |
| v.10-13 | **Worldwide chaos** | v.12-17 |

What are the responses that Jesus wants His followers to have during these times, based on Matthew 24:4, 6, 13, 14?

Matthew 24:14 introduces the preaching of the Gospel of the kingdom throughout the whole world, and this may well be where Revelation 7 fits in. God may use the sealed 144,000 Jews to share His word with the world, resulting in the salvation of multitudes. [132]

*Based on my understanding of Scripture, the events described above will not take place until after the church has been raptured. Rapture is imminent. It could come at any time. If it doesn't happen before the next lesson, we'll look at the verses that cause us to anticipate it!*

 Lesson Two: Matthew 24:15-35

# JESUS ANNOUNCES AN ABOMINATION

*Still here? Let's look at what we're anticipating to happen at anytime.*

Note the events that occur in the following verses:

**1 Corinthians 15:52**


**1 Thessalonians 4:15-17**


> Whenever someone mentions the Rapture, another is certain to point out that the word *rapture* never occurs in the Bible. While this is true, the concept of the Rapture is clearly present. The words "caught up" in 1 Thessalonians 4:17 translate from a Greek word (harpazo) that means "to snatch, to seize suddenly, or to transport from one place to another." It is also used of rescuing someone from a threatening danger (Acts 23:10, Jude 1:23). The translation of this Greek word into Latin is *rapturo*. That's where we get the English word *rapture* to describe this future event of being caught up to meet Jesus Christ in the clouds. [133]

*I spent a weekend in a seminary class taught by Dr. Charles Ryrie. Yes! The one who "wrote" the Ryrie Study Bible. He was passionate about prophecy and that's what our class was about. The final exam included this question: "What do you think is the strongest argument for pre-tribulational rapture?" That means – rapture occurring before the seven years of the Tribulation. My answer to that question (for which I received a check of approval!) was based on Revelation 3:10.*

What does Revelation 3:10 say?


*The "hour of testing" relates to Daniel 9:24 and 12:1 which describes a time of testing for the Jews which we call the Tribulation. Revelation 3 was written to the Philadelphian church, which means it was written to Christians, and they were told that they would be kept from the time of testing. Where is there no time? In heaven!*

*Rapture is the sudden descent of Jesus in the clouds and the calling up to heaven all who have believed in Him for salvation up to that point in time. Those who are "asleep" (dead) will be resurrected first and those who are alive will be caught up in the air where Jesus is. In the blink of an eye, all will be changed from tainted, decaying, mortal bodies to glorified, perfected, sanctified, eternal beings. I can't wait! Dr. Ryrie is in the presence of the Lord now, but I look forward to seeing him again in the air if rapture happens before I die!*

Based on this description of rapture and the description of events of the end-times from Matthew 24:4-14 in your chart, please make a simple timeline of things to come.

Look back at the responses Jesus told His disciples to have. You noted them above. If those are appropriate in the very worst of times, aren't they appropriate right now? Which, if any, do you need to apply to your current experiences?

*Are you ready to look closely at the things that are yet to come? We've had an overview of Jesus' final sermon and we've seen the general description of the time before His return. Now we will study the more detailed description of future events that He gives us. Bad news first. Then good news. Then... just be ready!*

**Please read Matthew 24:15-28.**

What did Daniel speak of? What are Jesus' followers to watch for?

What are they to do when they see it? How did Jesus emphasis the urgency of the situation?

Matthew 24:21 indicates a new situation. "For then" ...what?

And disciples are not to believe it when they hear... what?

*This passage in Matthew is a description of the Antichrist putting himself on the "throne" and ruling with evil intent against God's people, both the Jews and Jesus' disciples of that day.*

Matthew 24:15 is a direct quote of Daniel 9:27. The "code" in Daniel is that one day equals one year. So one week equals 7 years. Based on that timing, what does Daniel 9:27 tell you about the Antichrist and his rule?

What does 2 Thessalonians 2:3-4, 9-12 tell you about the Antichrist and his rule?

What does Revelation 13:11-18 tell you about the Antichrist and his rule?

*There are no words to describe how horrible this time will be. It is called the "great tribulation." The Antichrist will oppress the world more than any previous evil world ruler ever has. Nebuchadnezzar, Attila the Hun, and Adolf Hitler will seem like nice guys compared to him.*

*But there is good news!*

When does Matthew 24:29 say that things will change?

Very specific occurrences are stated in verses 29-31. Please list them.

---

There is nothing more clearly stated in the Bible than the fact that Jesus Christ is coming again. The second coming of Christ to this earth – His visible, literal, physical, glorious return – is explicitly referred to 1,845 times in the Bible. It is mentioned in twenty-three of the twenty-seven New Testament books. Christ Himself refers to His return twenty-one times in Scripture. [134]

---

*He's coming back! Just like He said He would! When? Matthew 24:29 tells us. How? Matthew 24:30 tells us. Where? (Hint: Matthew 24 and 25 are spoken there.)*

What does Acts 1:9-13 tell you about Jesus' return?

What does Zechariah 14:4 tell you about His return?

What does Zechariah 12:10-11 tell you about His return (compare this to Matthew 24:30)?

*I'd like to draw attention to Matthew 24:27-28 now. "For as the lightning comes from the east and flashes to the west, so also will the coming of the Son of Man be. For wherever the carcass is, there the eagles will be gathered together." The first sentence tells us that Jesus' return will be visible to all, rather than some secret appearance to a select few. And the mention of lightening indicates a sudden, striking, powerful approach. Then there's the strange mention of birds circling over dead meat. But the imagery in both of these statements coordinates perfectly with the awesome description of the triumphant return of Jesus Christ, King of Kings and Lord of Lords found in the book of the Revelation.*

**Please read Revelation 19:11-21.**

What are you most anticipating about the Second Coming of Christ?

*The "Parable of the Fig Tree" in Matthew 24:32-35 gives assurance that one day in the future, the generation of Jews and Gentiles alive at that time will see the events that He has described and they will know that His return is near. He declares the trustworthiness of His word which give all of us comfort that He is definitely coming back – some day!*

Lesson Three: Matthew 24:36-25:13

## JESUS PREPARES WITH PARABLES

Please pray for wisdom from the Holy Spirit to understand how to watch and wait for Jesus.

Look at your previous notes and make an updated timeline. Starting with rapture, add the end-time events that we have seen in Matthew 24:15-31. I place Matthew 24:4-14 in the first half of the 7 year tribulation, but you don't have to. (You can add events from the other passages if you like.)

*When will these things happen? What will happen? Those were the disciples' questions and Jesus has answered them.*

*What will you do until the end comes? That's what Jesus will emphasize in the remainder of His sermon. He is coming back. He guaranteed it. He has given general and specific indicators of when He will return. At some point in the future, people will see all the things that He spoke of; and they will see Him come on the clouds with great power and glory.*

What very important statement does Jesus make in Matthew 24:36?

*This is one of the most important things that Jesus tells us about the end of the age! The rest of the Olivet Discourse is related to this particular truth. Only God the Father knows when He will send Jesus the Son, the Messiah, back to earth. While the generation living then will see the signs of His coming, they will not be able to calculate the exact day and hour. The Weather Channel, NASA, and i-phone applications will all be inadequate for forecasting the return of the Christ.*

*No one knows exactly when Jesus is coming back to earth to judge the wicked, to reward the faithful, and to reign as King. Because 144,000 Jews will be saved and protected to preach the gospel (Rev. 7:4-9) and because the gospel will be preached to all the world (Matthew 24:14), we know that there will be disciples of Jesus during the seven years of the Tribulation before He returns. This means that while believers like you and me will have been raptured, there will be new believers on earth. It is to those believers that Jesus gives the following exhortations: be alert, be ready, and be faithful.*

**Read Matthew 24:36-42.**

**BE ALERT!**

What were people doing right up until the Flood arrived? What does this mean that life will be like during the Tribulation?

What did the flood do to those who were not ready for it? (Remember that the flood was God's judgment on the wicked.)

Based on what the flood did to those who were not saved in the ark, what will happen to individuals who are not ready for Jesus' return? (v. 41-42)

**Read Matthew 24:42-44**

**BE READY!**

How does Jesus' example in this passage tell people to be ready?

It goes without saying that Jesus was not comparing Himself in character to a thief but was comparing His coming to the stealth and unexpectedness of a thief's coming. In one sense, however, Jesus will come in the role as well as with the unexpectedness of a thief. As far as the ungodly are concerned, He will come and take away everything they have, all the things they have cherished and trusted in instead of Him. In this context, being ready seems to refer primarily to being saved, of being spiritually prepared to meet Christ as Lord and King rather than as Judge. [135]

**Read Matthew 24:45-51.**

**BE FAITHFUL!**

What does this example tell believers to do while anticipating the return of Jesus? What will be their reward?

How is the evil slave described in these verses?

Who will he join and what will be his outcome?

*Be alert. Watch for Jesus' return. Be ready. Be prepared to meet the Judge. Be faithful. Serve the Lord with the gifts and responsibilities that He has given you. These are the exhortations for Jesus' disciples at the end of the age during the Tribulation. But you can see that they are also the same instructions that we have been given throughout the book of Matthew. Whether the days are good or bad, easy or hard, short or long... we are to follow Jesus.*

Which of the exhortations above is the most challenging for you?

I hope you will find encouragement from James 5:8. What does it say?

*The wicked slave in Matthew 24:45-51 was not alert, prepared, or faithful for the unexpected return of his master. In that example, Jesus showed up earlier than expected. In the Parable of the Ten Virgins, we will see the problem that results from the opposite situation.*

**Read Matthew 25:1-13.**

This parable is an illustration of what, according to verse 1?

How were the five wise virgins ready for the bridegroom and what did they enjoy?

How were the other five virgins foolish? What happened to them in the end of the parable?

What is Jesus' conclusion to this parable?

*All of these illustrations from Jesus indicate that there will be those who are not prepared for His return as Judge and King. His Second Coming will surprise those who are more concerned about everyday tasks and pleasures than their salvation, just as the Flood surprised those in Noah's day. His Second Coming will surprise those who think they have time to live as they please, like the wicked servant. And His Second Coming will surprise those who say they are ready, but really aren't – like the foolish virgins.*

*In each of these scenarios, those who are not ready to meet Jesus the Judge and King will not be given a second chance to make a change. No one knows the day or hour of His return, but the time is now for repentance and salvation.*

*I've shared that I believe that the rapture will take place before the Tribulation and before the Second Coming of Jesus to the earth. The exhortations we have looked at in this lesson are specifically related to His Second Coming, but we should still be alert, ready, and faithful as we wait for the rapture of the church!*

*You looked at 1 Thessalonians 4:13-18 when we investigated the concept of rapture. Now look at Paul's very next words.*

How does Paul exhort believers in 1 Thessalonians 5:1-11? Just summarize!

How do the following verses encourage us to be prepared?

**Philippians 3:20**

**1 Thessalonians 1:10**

**Titus 2:11-13**

*The sermon on the Mount of Olives isn't over yet. Stay awake. We'll study some very familiar passages in our next lesson. You might be surprised at what you learn!*

Lesson Four: Matthew 25:13-46

## JESUS' CONCLUDING REMARKS

*In two days, Jesus will be handed over to the authorities to be crucified. He knows that time is short. We have His last words before us today before the final events of His life take place. What did He consider to be the most important things to communicate before His suffering?*

Pray that what is important to
Jesus will be important to you.

**Please read Matthew 25:13-30.**

This parable is an illustration of what, according to Matthew 25:1 and 14?

What does the master do in the following verses:

Verse 14

Verse 19

How do these actions relate to Jesus' Second Coming?

What do the servants do while the master is away and what are the consequences? Fill in the chart below.

| SERVANT | TALENTS | SERVANT'S ACTION | CONSEQUENCE |
|---------|---------|------------------|-------------|
| First   |         |                  |             |
| Second  |         |                  |             |
| Third   |         |                  |             |

Based on the opportunity given to the servants, and the commendation given to the first and second servants, what is the appropriate attitude and action to have while waiting for Jesus' Second Coming?

*The action and attitude of the third servant represent those who do not genuinely have faith in Jesus for salvation. His action was useless – producing absolutely nothing with what he had been given. His attitude was antagonistic toward his master, accusing him of being unmerciful (hard) and dishonest (gathering where he had sown no seed). The third servant had neither saving faith or works of faith. When the master settled accounts with him, the third servant had nothing.*

Does this parable trouble you or does it make sense?

What is Jesus' conclusion to the parable, in Matthew 25:29?

Those who demonstrate by their spiritual fruitfulness that they belong to God will be given even greater opportunity to bear fruit for Him. But those who demonstrate by their unproductiveness that they do not belong to God will lose even the benefits they once had. Such a person does not have any true blessings from God because he has made them worthless through disuse. But the reality of what those blessings could have been will be given to someone who has proved his genuineness. The divine principle is that those who trust in Christ will gain everything, and those who do not trust in Him will lose everything. [136]

*We have seen throughout the whole book of Matthew that both wheat and tares, good and bad, true and false, will exist together until the final day of judgment. It's the way things are now and the way things will be in the Tribulation. This is sad and sobering. It's also the subject of Jesus' final illustration.*

**Please read Matthew 25:31-46.**

When does this event take place?

What names and descriptions are given for Jesus in this passage? (See verses 31, 32, 34, 37, 40, 44.)

List the names of those separated on the right and left of Jesus and their descriptions.

**LEFT**                                                        **RIGHT**

Son of Man

On His Glorious Throne

All the angels with Him

Please look up the definition of the following word:
**Nations: Strong's #1484**
**Greek word:**
**Greek definition:**

To whom were the righteous from the nations ministering? Based on the context of Matthew 24 and 25, when would this ministry take place?

*I mentioned earlier that I attended a seminary class taught by Dr. Charles Ryrie. One assignment in the class was to answer the question below. I've included my answer which gives four options; the fourth option is my preference.*

QUESTION:

Who are the "brothers" to whom Jesus is referring in Matthew 25:40 when He says, "And the King will answer and say to them, 'Truly I say to you, to the extent that you did it to one of these brothers of Mine, even the least of them, you did it to Me'"?

POSSIBLE ANSWERS:

**1. The disciples.** If one considers the other references Jesus made to "his brothers," it is possible to understand them to be the disciples.

**2. Believers.** In several Scriptures, believers are called Jesus' brothers. Matt 12:50, Mark 3:35, Heb. 2:11-12

**3. Believing Jews during the Tribulation.** Some believe the term "brothers" has reference to Jews who are redeemed throughout the Tribulation.

**4. 144,000 sealed from every tribe of Israel.** The Jews who have been sealed during the Tribulation are the "brothers" to whom Christ is referring.

CONCLUSION:

According to Rev.7:1-8, God will save 144,000 Jews who will be faithful to Him and bear testimony to Him throughout the time of the Tribulation. These witnesses will be targets of the Beast's hatred, they will not bear his mark, and they will probably experience hunger, thirst, and imprisonment.[137] "So glorious and wonderful will be the ministry of the 144,000 saved Jews and so faithful will be their powerful testimony, the King on His throne of glory will not be ashamed to call them "My brothers." More than that, He will consider Himself so intimately united to them that what was done or not done to them is the same as being actually done or not done to Himself." [138] A Gentile who comes to the aid of one of the 144,000 sealed will be putting his life in danger. His assistance will be evidence of his faith in Jesus Christ, and so Jesus would gather that one to Himself as a sheep to inherit eternal life." [139]

*Following Jesus isn't a hard list of don't's. It's a heart list of do's.*

What are you doing for others in your present circumstances that gives evidence of your faith in Jesus Christ, the King?

The last words of Jesus' last sermon show His ultimate concern. What did He say in Matthew 25:46?

*There are only two types of people. Is that your ultimate concern?*

# JESUS' LAST DAYS

*It's time to walk through the last two days with Jesus. There is much suffering ahead. Jesus endured the cross by looking to the joy set before Him, and we can do the same. It is such a blessing to know that His death was not His final destiny.*

Please pray that the Holy Spirit will give you a desire to know Jesus more intimately.

**Please read Matthew 26:1-16.**

How do these four accounts indicate that Jesus' death is imminent?

Verses 1-2

Verses 3-5

Verses 6-13

Verses 14-16

Jesus announces His death, religious leaders plot His death, a woman anoints Him for His burial, and Judas betrays Him to His executioners. What does this tell you about God's sovereign control over the events?

**Please read Matthew 26:17-25.**

What does Jesus say on this occasion that indicates that His death is imminent?

How do the disciples respond when they hear that one of them is a betrayer?

*I've always thought it a little strange that Judas asked Jesus if he was the betrayer and equally strange to read Jesus' response to him. One commentary helped me see that Judas was still playing the hypocrite. He knew that he had already betrayed Jesus but feigned innocence and ignorance as the other disciples asked their questions with great concern. The commentary also said, "Jesus' response is a somewhat ambiguous affirmation, similar to the English idiom, 'you said it.' Without alerting the other disciples, this hints to Judas that Jesus is aware of his plot."* [140]

As soon as Judas had taken the bread, he went out. And it was night. John 13:30 [NIV]

*Judas was not a part of the rest of the meal.*

**Please read Matthew 26:26-30.**

What did Jesus do with the bread, and what was the significance of His action?

What did Jesus do with the wine, and what was the significance of His action?

How are believers today to remember this occasion, according to 1 Corinthians 11:23-29?

Matthew 26:28 is unique to the gospel accounts of the Last Supper. What does it say?

What does Jeremiah 31:31-34 teach you about the New Covenant? What will its impact be?

What does Hebrews 9:14-15 tell you regarding Jesus and the New Covenant?

What is the wonderful promise given in Matthew 26:29? (It's not about the wine!)

And when they had sung a hymn, they went out to the Mount of Olives. Matthew 26:30 ^NKJ

*The Passover meal traditionally ended with songs of praise to the Lord for deliverance out of the bondage of Egypt. Jesus' giving of His body and His blood would bring about deliverance out of bondage to sin and death, and while there was great suffering still to be endured, there was great joy in store for Jesus and all of His disciples throughout history. It was appropriate to sing a hymn of praise.*

*The Hallel psalms were probably sung at the Passover meal, and Psalm 118 is considered the climax of that group of psalms.*

Please read Psalm 118. Note a few of the verses that are meaningful to you.

*Deliverance would come. Soon. However, denial by the disciples would come first.*

**Please read Matthew 26:31-35.**

*It sounds like that was a conversation just between Jesus and Peter. All the disciples chimed eventually though.*

What did Jesus explain – twice?

How did Peter answer – twice?

What was the good news given by Jesus in the middle of the troubling announcement?

*It can be very hard to absorb good news when you're in the midst of trials. I know the Holy Spirit reminded the disciples of all that Jesus had told them. We need Him to do the same for us.*

Let's go back to the good news that Jesus gave us in His very first sermon. What do you need to be reminded of today, from Matthew 5:3-12?

*It's getting later and darker on this night that we are reading about. That describes the hour and the lighting as well as the timing and the trouble. We'll pause here as Jesus and the disciples make their way to the Garden of Gethsemane. We'll meet them there in our next lesson.*

Lesson Six: Matthew 26:36-75

# JESUS SURRENDERS HIS WILL

*Walk down through the valley; then climb up the hill. There's a grove of olive trees which was familiar territory for Jesus and His disciples. It's Gethsemane – this word is probably from the Aramaic "gath shemānīm," which means oil press. In this place, olives would be gathered into a huge stone mortar and pressed under a great stone wheel. Intense pressure and repeated crushing produced the precious olive oil. This is what Jesus endured in this place as well.*

Please pray for the Spirit to lead you to a deeper
appreciation for the sacrifice of Christ.

**Please read Matthew 26:36-46.**

What did Jesus experience here?

> The mystery of the agony of God's unique Son cannot be fully penetrated. [141]

What did the disciples experience here?

Jesus agonized in prayer and repeated His specific request three times. What did He say?

> To drink of a cup, in the Scriptures, often signifies to be afflicted, or to be punished (Isa.51:17, Isa.51:22; Psalm 73:10; Psalm 75:8; Jer. 25:15; Rev. 16:9). The figure is taken from a feast, where the master of a feast extends a cup to those present. Thus God is represented as extending to his Son a cup filled with a bitter mixture — one causing deep sufferings. [142]

What do Jesus' prayers tell you about His relationship to His Father?

*Sometimes I readily yield to God's will for me. But many times, I struggle with submission. Jesus' prayers to His Father have been the example that I have followed to come to the point of surrender.*

Have you prayed, or do you need to pray now – "not as I will, but as You will"?

*This was the last time that the disciples would be with Jesus before His death and resurrection. Matthew has been showing us through his narratives that they were oblivious to Jesus' impending death despite His repeated declarations that the time had come. Now, in the garden, when they were specifically called upon to be alert and pray with Jesus, they fell asleep.*

What is the lesson that we should learn from Matthew 26:40-41?

Can the spirit overcome the flesh? How do the following verses encourage you?

**1 Corinthians 16:13**


**Ephesians 6:18**


**Colossians 4:2**


"Could you not watch with Me one hour?" Have you ever prayed for an hour – either with someone or alone? Write out a list, or a schedule, of what you could pray for during one hour. (Then set aside an hour this week to do so.)


*The pain and suffering have begun. Jesus has accepted the Father's plan. While He repeatedly declared that no one knows the timing of the return of the Son of Man, He demonstrates that He is fully aware of the timing of His death and departure.*

How does Matthew 26:45-46 show Jesus' acceptance and awareness of the Father's plan?


**Please read Matthew 26:47-56.**

What surprises you, or seems strange to you, in this account of Jesus' betrayal and arrest?


*It's late at night. It's dark. Jesus and His disciples are quiet in a privately owned olive garden. And then there is a great multitude with swords and clubs! Judas. A kiss! Jesus calls him friend! They seize Jesus. And Peter cuts somebody's ear off.*

What does Matthew emphasize in Matthew 26:52-56? What important points are made? What is repeated?


*Then all the disciples forsook Him and fled. Just like He said they would.*

**Please read Matthew 26:57-68.**

What was the goal of the council? What problem did they have?

> This hearing exhibits anything but the impartiality and fairness mandated by Scripture and Jewish law. [143]

*Finally, somebody came forward and misquoted Jesus. The high priest wanted Jesus to refute the false witness and entrap Himself. But He said nothing.*

What did the high priest specifically ask Jesus?

How did Jesus respond?

*Jesus' answer was a combination of Psalm 110:1 and Daniel 7:13, clearly affirming that He is the Messiah, the Son of Man, the Son of God. "Power" stands for God by metonymy. This is the ultimate statement thus far in Matthew of Jesus' identity as the Christ. "Nowhere does Jesus reveal Himself more than here." [144]*

What is the appropriate response to this revelation of Jesus' identity? How do you respond?

How did the high priest and council react to Jesus' declaration?

What is your reaction to their actions?

How are we to follow Jesus' example according to 1 Peter 2:20-23?

**Please read Matthew 26:69-75.**

*You have probably noticed that we move quickly through some passages. We're keeping our eyes fixed on Jesus, the author and perfecter of our faith, who for the joy set before Him, endured the cross, scorning its shame.*

How does Matthew draw attention to Jesus in the passage you just read?

*Jesus knows His disciples. Jesus knows us. He knows our weaknesses and just as He warned Peter, so His word warns us as well. We are as susceptible to denying our Lord as Peter was.*

What encouragement and warning are given in 2 Timothy 2:12-13?

What's another way of denying Jesus, according to Titus 1:16?

Are you denying Jesus in any way right now?

> The early church made the crowing rooster a symbol of watchfulness and vigilance. It reminded Christians of Peter's denial and repentance. In this way the crowing rooster became one of the symbols of the crucifixion. Early paintings of the apostle Peter show him holding the keys of heaven with a rooster pictured nearby to remind us of his denial. But the rooster does more than recall Peter's denial; it causes us to think of our susceptibility to pride, our fear of standing up for Christ, and our vulnerability to denying Christ. [145]

# The Most Important Part

## Matthew 27:1 — 28:20

# JESUS DIES

*The night is over. The secret council has ended. Jesus has been sentenced to death. The Jews just need the Romans to execute Him.*

Please pray that you will want to know the fellowship of Christ's sufferings.

**Please read Matthew 27:1-2.**

What has just happened to Jesus, according to this account?

**Please read Matthew 27:3-9.**

What has just happened to Judas, according to this account?

Why do you think Matthew included this information about Judas? What is his conclusion to the narrative?

**Please read Matthew 27:11-26.**

Record each description that Pilate and his wife give of Jesus.

Why was Pilate amazed at Jesus?

*He did not speak up in His own defense. He did not declare His innocence or His identity. Some might have declared Him insane. He was either lunatic, liar, or Lord. The Jews decided that He was a liar. A blasphemer. From their perspective, that was what was in their best interest.*

How did Jesus' trial before Pilate end? What was the verdict and the outcome?

> Flogging was a horrible, flesh-ripping experience that hastened the death of those about to be crucified. The victim was tied to a post or forced to the ground. The scourge was a short whip that had several leather thongs with lead balls and sharp pieces of bone or metal attached to them. Such horrendous punishment would cause deep lacerations of the back, severe pain, and loss of blood. [146]

**Please read Matthew 27:27-32.**

What did the Roman soldiers do to Jesus?




*This was intended as a cruel parody of royalty. Mocking. Jesting. Insulting. I find it disgusting. It was, however, another fulfillment of Jesus' own prophecy: "the Son of Man will be betrayed to the chief priests and to the scribes; and they will condemn Him to death, and deliver Him to the Gentiles to mock and to scourge and to crucify." Matthew 20:18-19*

What did the Roman soldiers do to Simon of Cyrene?




> Normally a condemned criminal is forced to carry his own cross. Although practices varied, carrying the cross normally involved only the horizontal crossbar. The vertical stake was already erected at the site of execution. [147]

*According to Matthew, Mark, and Luke, Jesus did not carry the cross. This is another indication of Jesus' innocence.*

**Please read Matthew 27:33-44.**

> Crucifixion epitomized cruel and unusual punishment.... Long nails were frequently driven through the victim's ankles into the vertical post of the cross and through the victim's outstretched hands or wrists into the horizontal beam.... The medical cause(s) of death by crucifixion would be asphyxia, loss of blood, dehydration, and/or shock. [148]

*"Then they crucified Him..."*

What is your reaction to the violent abuse and suffering that Jesus experienced?

*Matthew's account of the crucifixion is surprisingly matter-of-fact. He draws attention to how seemingly incidental occurrences fulfill the Scriptures. And above all, he continues to highlight the true identity of Jesus.*

Who said what about Jesus that indicated that He was the Messiah, even if they didn't believe it themselves?

*This is the moment for which Jesus was born. The moment for which He had lived. The moment which all the world desperately needed.*

**Please read Matthew 27:45-56.**

What eternally important events happened in the following verses?

Verse 45

Verse 46

Verse 50

Verse 51

How does 2 Corinthians 5:21 explain what Jesus experienced?

*Hallelujah! What a Savior! Amazing love. Oh what sacrifice. The Son of God, given for me. My death He died, and my life He lives.... That I might live.*

What do you want to say to the One who died for you?

# JESUS LIVES!

*The darkest day of history is over. One life has changed many lives for eternity. We know it, but those who watched Jesus die didn't know it yet.*

Please pray that you will know
the power of Christ's resurrection.

**Please read Matthew 27:57-61.**

How did Joseph of Arimathea honor Jesus and why?

What do you think about what he did?

**Please read Matthew 27:62-66.**

What were the chief priests and Pharisees worried about and why?

*Matthew reminds us through the words of the religious leaders that Jesus had said "after three days I will rise." At this point in his narrative, Jesus is dead but His words are still true! The leaders can seal up the tomb and set a guard, but it won't matter.*

*The first day passes. The second day passes. The third day...He rose! Up from the grave He arose! With a mighty triumph over His foes! He arose a victor from the dark domain and He lives forever with His saints to reign.... He arose! He arose! Praise God, Jesus Christ arose!*

**Please read Matthew 28:1-10.**

Ha! What happened to that securely sealed tomb and the guards?

What is the good news that the angel gave the women?

*These words are life-changing!*

What impact did they have on the women?

What difference do they make according to 1 Peter 1:3-4?

How was Jesus raised and what else happened according to Ephesians 1:19-23?

*It was good news when the women were told that Jesus had risen from the dead. But it was even better when they saw Him!*

What happened in Matthew 28:9?

*Can you imagine that moment? Oh! The women must have been completely overwhelmed with emotion. And Jesus gave them permission to rejoice! To be glad! To celebrate! And touch Him! And worship Him! By the way, Matthew's comment about the women touching Him indicates to us that Jesus' body was physically resurrected! I know that we can't physically see Jesus or touch Him at this point in time, but it is possible to meet Him through the pages of the Bible.*

How do you meet with Jesus and rejoice in His presence and worship Him?

*Jesus told the women – don't be afraid. "The women are probably still afraid because of the extraordinary events they have just encountered, and the appearance of Jesus escalates their apprehension. Events are unfolding at a pace that outstrips their ability to maintain their grip."[149] That's right! Mary and Mary Magdalene experienced one surprise after another. Life can be like that when you see Jesus! He graciously reminded them of their mission.*

*"Go and tell My brethren to go to Galilee and there they will see Me." Go and tell! So that others will see Him too! We must do the same.*

Believing in the resurrection of Jesus Christ is not optional. Why, according to 1 Corinthians 15:17-20?

**Please read Matthew 28:11-15.**

That's a conspiracy theory for sure. Did it work?

**Please read Matthew 28:16-20.**

How many disciples went to Galilee? Why is that number important?



*One commentary says: "They found themselves in a state of cognitive dissonance par excellence."* [150] *The disciples worshipped Jesus, but some doubted. The word doubt does not mean unbelief or perplexity, but hesitation, uncertainty, or indecision.*

*This strange comment from Matthew is actually the introduction to the command from Jesus. The One with all authority is going to wipe away all uncertainty.*

**Based on Matthew 28:18-20:**

What does Jesus want the disciples to know about Himself?



> The conclusion of any book, letter, or treatise usually contains an explicit statement or summary of the author's purpose for writing; Matthew is no exception. The resurrection does not happen for its own sake, and Matthew's gospel does not end, therefore, with the resurrection; it ends with the Great Commission of world-wide mission. [151]


What's the mission?



*While this is a mission, it is even more so a passion. It's all about knowing a holy God, enjoying a saving relationship with Jesus Christ, and sharing it with others.*

What are the three steps of making disciples?



How are the three persons of the Trinity identified as one?



How does Jesus describe His relationship with His disciples now?



How would you describe your relationship with Jesus now?

# FINAL REFLECTIONS

*What a journey it has been – to spend time with Jesus and His disciples. Up and down and all around the land of Israel. Through the good times and the bad times. Hearing words of encouragement and words of great challenge and conviction.*

> I pray that the grace of the Lord Jesus Christ,
> and the love of God,
> and the fellowship of the Spirit will be with you.

I'd like you for you to reflect on what we've heard and seen in the book of Matthew. Look at the titles of our lessons on the Table of Contents page. Turn to and review a few lessons that you remember as being particularly meaningful to you. How has this study on the life of Jesus impacted your life?

*I like to end my studies with God's inspired words rather than my own. I've noted on this page and the next, in reverse order, a few verses from Matthew. Highlight some that are your favorites.*

**Matthew 22:37-40**   Jesus said to him, " 'You shall love the LORD your God with all your heart, with all your soul, and with all your mind.' ³⁸This is the first and great commandment. ³⁹And the second is like it: 'You shall love your neighbor as yourself.' ⁴⁰On these two commandments hang all the Law and the Prophets."

**Matthew 16:24**   Then Jesus said to His disciples, "If anyone desires to come after Me, let him deny himself, and take up his cross, and follow Me."

**Matthew 13:11**   He answered and said to them, "Because it has been given to you to know the mysteries of the kingdom of heaven, but to them it has not been given."

**Matthew 11:28-30**   "Come to Me, all you who labor and are heavy laden, and I will give you rest. ²⁹Take My yoke upon you and learn from Me, for I am gentle and lowly in heart, and you will find rest for your souls. ³⁰For My yoke is easy and My burden is light."

**Matthew 9:35-38**   Then Jesus went about all the cities and villages, teaching in their synagogues, preaching the gospel of the kingdom, and healing every sickness and every disease among the people. 36But when He saw the multitudes, He was moved with compassion for them, because they were weary and scattered, like sheep having no shepherd. 37Then He said to His disciples, "The harvest truly is plentiful, but the laborers are few. 38Therefore pray the Lord of the harvest to send out laborers into His harvest."

**Matthew 7:24**   "Therefore whoever hears these sayings of Mine, and does them, I will liken him to a wise man who built his house on the rock."

**Matthew 7:29**   ...for He taught them as one having authority, and not as the scribes.

**Matthew 4:19**   Then He said to them, "Follow Me, and I will make you fishers of men."

**Matthew 3:16-17**   When He had been baptized, Jesus came up immediately from the  water; and behold, the heavens were opened to Him, and He saw the Spirit of God  descending like a dove and alighting upon Him. 17And suddenly a voice came from heaven, saying, "This is My beloved Son, in whom I am well pleased."

**Matthew 1:21-23**   "And she will bring forth a Son, and you shall call His name JESUS, for He will save His people from their sins." 22So all this was done that it might be fulfilled which was spoken by the Lord through the prophet, saying, 23"Behold, the virgin shall be with child, and bear a Son, and they shall call His name Immanuel," which is translated, "God with us."

**Matthew 1:16**   And Jacob begot Joseph the husband of Mary, of whom was born Jesus who is called Christ.

*Follow Him.*

# Endnotes

1. Warren Wiersbe, *Be Loyal,* p.6, *Cook Communications, Colorado Springs, 2004.*
2. Jamieson, Robert, A.R. Fausset, David Brown, *A commentary, critical and explanatory, on the whole Bible, with introduction to Old Testament literature, a pronouncing dictionary of Scripture proper names, tables of weights and measures, and an index to the entire Bible.* George H. Doran Co., New York, 1921.
3. J. Dwight Pentecost, *The Words and Works of Jesus Christ*, p.55, *Zondervan, Grand Rapids, MI, 1981.*
4. Pentecost, p. 70.
5. Pentecost, p.83.
6. *Theological Wordbook of the Old Testament,* 1879.0 צדק , Bibleworks Software.
7. Barclay Newman Greek English Dictionary, Bibleworks, 1600 δικαιοσύνη
8. William D. Mounce, *Basics of Biblical Greek*, p. 225. *Zondervan, Grand Rapids, MI, 2003.*
9. James Montgomery Boice, *The Gospel of Matthew*, p. 64. *Baker Books, Grand Rapids, MI, 2007.*
10. Boice, p. 66,67.
11. John MacArthur, *The MacArthur New Testament Commentary: Matthew*, p.125. *Moody Press, Chicago, 1989.*
12. Macarthur, p.136, 141.
13. Macarthur, p. 138.
14. Donald A. Hagner, *Word Biblical Commentary,* p.91. *Word, Incorporated, 1995.*
15. David L. Turner, *Baker Exegetical Commentary on the New Testament: Matthew*, p. 147. *Baker Academic, Grand Rapids, MI, 2008.*
16. Turner, p. 150.
17. Turner, p. 151.
18. Turner, p. 152-153.
19. Michael J. Wilkins, *The NIV Application Commentary: Matthew*, p. 213. *Zondervan, Grand Rapids, MI, 2004.*
20. Wilkins, p. 215.
21. Smith, William, *Smith's Bible Dictionary,* Hendrickson Publishers, Peabody, Massachusetts, 2002.
22. Hagner, p. 134.
23. Hagner, p. 134.
24. MacArthur, p. 379.
25. Hagner, p. 152.
26. Boice, p. 106.
27. Turner, p.200.
28. Wiersbe, p. 49.
29. *Vincent Word Studies*, Matthew 7:6, www.e-sword.net.
30. Hagner, p. 177.
31. Hagner, p. 177.
32. Hagner, p. 188.
33. Macarthur, p. 487.
34. *Vincent Word Studies,* Matthew 7:27.
35. J.K. Johnston, Why Christians Sin, Discovery House, 1992, p. 121.
36. *Words:* J. Wilbur Chapman, 1910. *Music:* Hyfrydol, Rowland H. Prichard, 1830
37. Turner, p. 240.
38. Pentecost, p. 155.
39. Pentecost, p. 155.
40. MacArthur, p. 70.
41. Wilkins, p. 372.
42. Turner, p. 261.
43. MacArthur , p. 103.
44. Turner, p. 262.
45. MacArthur
46. Tim Hansel, Eating Problems for Breakfast, Word Publishing, 1988, pp. 194-195.
47. D. A. Carson, "2. The commission (10:5b-16)" In *The Expositor's Bible Commentary*: Volume 8. 245. Zondervan Publishing House, Grand Rapids, 1984.
48. Carson, Matthew 10:5b-16.
49. Boice, p. 178.
50. Carson, Matthew 10 23.
51. Carson, Matthew 10:26-27
52. *Vincent Word Studies* , Matthew 10:34.
53. Barbara Friberg, Timothy Friberg, Neva F. Miller, *Analytical Lexicon of the Greek New Testament*, Baker Books, Grand Rapids, 2000,Bibleworks Software, lambano.
54. *Thayer's Greek Definitions*, #2983 –take, www.e-sword.net.
55. Bromily, Geoffrey William, *International Standard Bible Encyclopedia*, Eerdmans, Grand Rapids, Michigan, 1979.
56. Living in the Times of Jesus of Nazareth, Peter Connolly, 1983, Steimatzky Td, Bnei Brak, Israel
57. http://www.npr.org/templates/story/story.php?storyId=125486910
58. http://en.wikipedia.org/wiki/Eureka_(word)
59. Hagner
60. Turner, p.292.
61. Carson, Matthew 11:25-26.
62. Carson, Matthew 11:25-26.
63. Turner, p. 304.
64. Hagner, p. 320.
65. MacArthur, p. 277.
66. Alfred Edersheim, *The Life and Times of Jesus the Messiah*, Grand Rapids: Wm. B. Eerdmans Publishing, Co., 1971 [orig. 1883], vol. I, pp. 267-270.
67. Turner, p.305.
68. MacArthur, p. 275.
69. Edersheim, p. 508
70. Carson, Matthew 12:15-21.
71. MacArthur, p. 311.
72. MacArthur, p. 311.
73. Carson, Matthew 12:46-50.
74. Bromily, Tares.
75. MacArthur, p. 367.
76. Don Sandberg, Handout: 12 facts about the Parables of Jesus, 2010.
77. Turner, p. 353.
78. MacArthur, p. 396.
79. MacArthur, p. 399.
80. Turner, p. 360.

81. Barnes, Albert, *Albert Barnes Notes on the Bible,* Matthew 8:11, www.e-sword.net.
82. Hagner, p. 419.
83. See the Morning: *Enough,* by Chris Tomlin and Louis Giglio.
84. Turner, p. 373.
85. G. K. Beale and D. A . Carson, *Commentary on the New Testament Use of the Old Testament,* p. 50, Baker Academic, Grand Rapids, 2007.
86. From *The Nelson Study Bible,* p.1601, copyright © 1997 by Thomas Nelson, Inc. Used by permission.
*87.* John Charles Ryle, *Expository Thoughts on the Gospels: St. Matthew,* p. 174, James Clarke, Cambridge, 1974.
88. Turner, p. 388.
89. Hagner, p. 450.
90. Turner, p. 393.
*91.* Turner, p. 397.
92. Hagner, p. 463.
93. Hagner, p. 469.
94. Turner, p. 406.
95. Wiersbe, p. 113.
96. Hagner, p. 480.
97. From *The Nelson Study Bible,* p.1605, copyright © 1997 by Thomas Nelson, Inc. Used by permission.
98. Wilkins, p. 596.
99. Wilkins, p. 597.
100. Wilkins, p. 613.
101. Turner, p. 292.
102. Turner, p. 443.
103. MacArthur, p. 137.
104. MacArthur, p. 137.
105. Turner, p. 450.
106. From *The Nelson Study Bible,* p.1608, copyright © 1997 by Thomas Nelson, Inc. Used by permission.
107. Hagner, p. 549.
108. *Theological Wordbook of the Old Testament,* 1273- naaph.
109. Hagner, p. 559.
110. I surrender all - hymn
111. Turner, p. 472.
112. Toussaint, p. 228.
113. Turner, p. 479.
114. Wilkins, p. 668.
115. Hagner, p. 581.
*116. Thayer's Greek Definitions,* www.e-sword.net.
117. Turner, p. 504.
118. Wilkins, p. 696.
119. Turrner, p. 516.
120. Turner, p. 525.
121. Wilkins, p. 718.
122. Wilkins, p. 718.
123. Turner, p. 532.
124. Turner, p. 542.
125. Barnes, Matthew 23:4.
126. Bromily
127. Wilkins, p. 748.
128. Wilkins, p. 749.
129. Wilkins, p. 749.
130. Friberg, 20023 – woe.
131. Turner, p. 561.
132. Wiersbe
133. Mark Hitchcock, *The Complete Book of Bible Prophecy,* p. 42, Tyndale House Publishers, Wheaton, 1999.
134. Hitchcock, p. 70.
135. MacArthur, p. 77.
136. MacArthur , p. 108.
137. Pentecost, p. 410.
138. Unger Merrill F. Unger, *Beyond the Crystal Ball* (Chicago, IL: Moody Press, 1973), pp. 134-35. (taken from Pre-trib Research Center Article, Posttribulationism and the Sheep/Goat-Judgment of Matthew 25 — A Summary-Critique of Robert Gundry's View, by Dr. Ron Rhodes)
139. *Bible Knowledge Commentary,* Matthew 25:31-40. Walvoord and Zuck, eds., Victor Books, 1989.
140. Turner, p. 625.
141. Hagner, p.785.
142. Barnes
143. Turner, p. 639.
144. Hagner, p.799.
145. Douglas D. Webster, *The Discipline of Surrender: Biblical Images of Discipleship,* Intervarsity Press, Downers Grove, Illinois, 2001, p.80.
146. Turner, p. 655.
147. Turner, p. 659.
148. Turner, p. 665.
149. Wilkins, p. 941.
150. Hagner, p. 885.
151. Wilkins, p. 970.

# SUGGESTED RESOURCES

*Shepherd's Notes: Matthew.* Dana Gould, editor. © 1997 by B & H Publishing Group, Nashville, TN.

*The Strongest Strong's Exhaustive Concordance* by James Strong — available through online resources below and Google

## Suggested (free) online study helps:
*These include various Bible translations and links to all resources mentioned below.*

**studylight.org  searchgodsword.org   blueletterbible.org**

**e-sword.net** (free program to download, then available offline)

*The following list includes study helps that are available for free online if you are interested in pursuing more information about the Scriptures on your own. Descriptions are from e-sword.net.*

## Commentaries:
### Robertson's Word Pictures in the New Testament
Robertson's magnum opus has a reputation as one of the best New Testament word study sets. Providing verse-by-verse commentary, it stresses meaningful and pictorial nuances implicit in the Greek but often lost in translation. And for those who do not know Greek, exegetical material and interpretive insights are directly connected with studies in the original text. All Greek words are transliterated.

### Treasury of Scriptural Knowledge
This classic Bible study help gives you a concordance, chain-reference system, topical Bible and commentary all in one! Turn to any Bible passage, and you'll find chapter synopses, key word cross-references, topical references, parallel passages and illustrative notes that show how the Bible comments on itself. This really is a treasure!

### Vincent's Word Studies
Marvin Vincent's Word Studies has been treasured by generations of pastors and laypeople. Commenting on the meaning, derivation, and uses of significant Greek words and idioms, Vincent helps you incorporate the riches of the New Testament in your sermons or personal study without spending hours on tedious language work!

### John Gill's Exposition of the Entire Bible
Having preached in the same church as C. H. Spurgeon, John Gill is little known, but his works contain gems of information found nowhere outside of the ancient Jewish writings. John Gill presents a verse-by-verse exposition of the entire Bible.

## Jamieson, Fausset and Brown Commentary

Long considered one of the best conservative commentaries on the entire Bible, the JFB Bible Commentary offers practical insight from a reformed evangelical perspective. The comments are an insightful balance between learning and devotion, with an emphasis on allowing the text to speak for itself.

## Keil & Delitzsch Commentary on the Old Testament

This commentary is a classic in conservative biblical scholarship! Beginning with the nature and format of the Old Testament, this evangelical commentary examines historical and literary aspects of the text, as well as grammatical and philological issues. Hebrew words and grammar are used, but usually in content, so you can follow the train of thought.


# Dictionaries:

## Easton's Bible Dictionary

Easton's Bible Dictionary provides informative explanations of histories, people and customs of the Bible. An excellent and readily understandable source of information for the student and layperson. This dictionary is one of Matthew George Easton's most significant literary achievements.

## International Standard Bible Encyclopedia

This authoritative reference dictionary explains every significant word in the Bible and Apocrypha! Learn about archaeological discoveries, the language and literature of Bible lands, customs, family life, occupations, and the historical and religious environments of Bible people.

## Smith's Bible Dictionary

A classic reference, this comprehensive Bible dictionary gives you thousands of easy-to-understand definitions, verse references and provides a wealth of basic background information that you'll find indispensable as you read the Bible.

## Thayer's Greek Definitions

For over a century, Joseph Henry Thayer's Greek-English Lexicon of the New Testament has been lauded as one of the finest available! Based on the acclaimed German lexicon by C.L.W. Grimm, Thayer's work adds comprehensive extra-biblical citations and etymological information, expanded references to other works, increased analysis of textual variations, and discussion of New Testament synonyms. An invaluable resource for students of New Testament Greek!

## Noah Webster's Dictionary of American English

Noah Webster once wrote, "Education is useless without the Bible." That's why his first dictionary is the only one available today that defines every word in the original language and its biblical usage. Compare Webster's definitions of words like "marriage" and "education" with those found in modern dictionaries, and see the difference for yourself!

# PRAYER REQUESTS
## AND PRAISES

*Do not be anxious about anything, but in everything, by prayer and petition, with thanksgiving, present your requests to God. Philippians 4:6 [NIV]*

# PRAYER REQUESTS AND PRAISES

*As for me, far be it from me that I should sin against the LORD by failing to pray for you.* **1 Samuel 12:23** *NIV*

# PRAYER REQUESTS
## AND PRAISES

*Let us therefore come boldly to the throne of grace, that we may obtain mercy and find grace to help in time of need. Hebrews 4:16 KJV*

# PRAYER REQUESTS AND PRAISES

*I pray that out of His glorious riches He may strengthen you with power through His Spirit in your inner being. Ephesians 3:16 NIV*

# PRAYER REQUESTS AND PRAISES

*We can be confident that He will listen to us whenever we ask for anything in line with His will and... we can be sure that He will give us what we ask for. 1 John 5:14-15 NLT*

# PRAYER REQUESTS
## AND PRAISES

*Let us come before His presence with thanksgiving,*
*and let us shout joyfully to Him with psalms. Psalms 95:2 NKJ*

# Prayer requests
## and praises

*Then you will call upon Me and come and pray to Me, and I will listen to you.*
*Jeremiah 29:12* [NIV]

# PRAYER REQUESTS
## AND PRAISES

*...the Spirit Himself makes intercession for us with groanings which cannot be uttered.*
*Romans 8:26* ^NIV

# PRAYER REQUESTS
## AND PRAISES

*Jesus looked at them and said, "With man this is impossible, but not with God; all things are possible with God." Mark 10:27 NIV*